Profitable Problem Solving
Bridgette Chambers

EmpoweredW Press
www.empoweredwpress.com

EmpoweredW Press
ISBN 13: 978-0692435557
ISBN 10: 0692435557

To contact Bridgette Chambers:
info@profitableproblemsolving.com

Profitableproblemsolving.com

"Our greatness lies not so much in being able to remake the world … as in being able to remake ourselves."

                                          -Mahatma Gandhi

The book is dedicated to Brenda, Matthew, and Michelle. Thank you for the love that allows a person to constantly follow her dreams and ambitions.

Table of Contents

Introduction

In today's ever-changing business world, there's one thing that remains the same: people's fascination with entrepreneurs. We're excited by the Sara Blakelys and Richard Bransons and Mark Zuckerbergs of the world, starting with very little and riding their entrepreneurial drive (and a streak of good luck along the way) to Spanx, Virgin, and Facebook. We can't make ourselves look away from Donald Trump. Reality television shows like *Shark Tank* and *The Big Fix* are proof of our fixation with the entrepreneurial mindset, the problem-solving intellect, and the drama inherent in business success.

Our grandparents gobbled up the Horatio Alger stories of rags to riches. We cheer for Rudy, Rocky, Forrest Gump, and Seabiscuit for the same reasons we watch *Restaurant Impossible* and *Undercover Boss.* We Americans have a long-standing love affair with the classic underdog. It's part of our national character. Every one of us believes that we, too, have it in us to defy odds and achieve our dreams.

Of all the business success stories, the grandest is the corporate turnaround. It's our own fairytale, writ large. It's the ultimate heroic story, isn't it?

Well, no.

Not really.

Look at it this way. Every turnaround—whether successful or failed—shares one common factor: the company wouldn't need a turnaround if it hadn't already missed countless opportunities to remediate and restore operational readiness, quality, profitability, market share, or whatever benchmark is the primary indicator of trouble for the company.

In other words, if the company had identified and solved its problems earlier, when they were simple and less disruptive, the turnaround wouldn't have been necessary.

That's what this book is about: identifying and solving problems. In these pages, I will be dealing with a two-pronged process, performed from two different directions by players who are *in this together*. The corporate CEO and other top management create a corporate culture of innovation, problem-solving, and *continuous improvement*; employees at all levels of the corporation are empowered to identify problems, solve them, and add value to the company—and they are rewarded for doing so.

I call this process *Profitable Problem Solving*.

I have made use of all these principles throughout my career as a sales leader on the rise, a CEO, and an accomplished turnaround specialist. I believe that employees at all levels (and the corporations they serve) can benefit from applying them.

I like to think of Profitable Problem Solving as a soccer game.

Imagine two teams going at it furiously on the soccer field. The opponent steals the ball from your forward, maneuvers past your midfielders and fullbacks, and is now driving toward your goalkeeper. The fans hold their breath. The keeper tenses, preparing to leap to the right or the left. The opponent swings back her foot and prepares to shoot.

There are two possible outcomes. The opponent's incredible shot flies past the goalkeeper and wins the game. Or, if your team is lucky, your goalkeeper's incredible save stops the opponent's winning goal. I played keeper for many years and can tell you, even when you're a rock star, there will be important balls that get past you.

A company's ability to solve problems before the issues score points for its competitors has much in common with our soccer team.

The ball got past one defender after another, until it became a critical risk for the team. It wasn't the sole fault of any one player, but there were numerous moments in which one of your players could have stolen back the ball and prevented the crisis. If your goalkeeper fails to defend the goal, it's not just the goalkeeper's fault. The entire team has failed.

Likewise, if a company underperforms—lacking liquidity, stability, profitability, quality, and market share—then the entire team shares the blame. If a company reaches the point where it desperately needs a turnaround, then the ball has gotten past the entire team. There were numerous moments when someone—the CEO, an entry-level new hire, or anyone in between—could have recognized the problem, come up with a solution, and solved the issue. At an early stage (way back there among the midfielders and fullbacks), the company could have solved the problem with a minimum of disruption. But now (with the goalkeeper tensed to make a desperate save), you can bet that repairing the damage is going to be very unpleasant.

More times than not, when turning around an organization or division, I've had to drastically cut expenses in order to restore enough working capital to fund the turnaround. Usually, and I say this with regret, this means cutting labor expenses. If you have not had the gut-wrenching experience of letting talented people go, you should thank your lucky stars. It's painful to let talented people go, especially when they are working hard for a company that simply cannot afford its own operations.

Clearly, when a company reaches the point where it needs a turnaround, requiring layoffs, early retirements, and massive restructuring, the ball got past the entire team.

But what if you could turn back time? What if the CEO had empowered those talented, dedicated people to identify problems before they became costly? What if the company had remediated the issues while the solutions were still affordable and minimally disruptive?

And, what if everyone in the company, from the CEO to the division managers to the folks on the manufacturing floor, had changed their perspective just a few degrees? What if they had all looked at problems as opportunities, rather than annoyances or obstacles?

For the CEO, solving problems is how she puts her own mark on the company, builds a successful corporate culture, and makes a name for herself. When the CEO solves problems in a grand, transparent way, employees, stakeholders, customers, and the market take notice and respond.

For the employee, solving problems is how she differentiates herself from her colleagues who are merely fulfilling their job descriptions. If there are no problems, then there are no challenges. If she does just what's in her job description, but nothing more, then her entrepreneurial skills, creativity, and enthusiasm go to waste.

But if she pictures herself in cleats on our soccer field, with problems surrounding her, then she'll have abundant opportunities to show her stuff.

The corporation in which everyone celebrates challenges is most often a corporation that is agile, nimble, innovative, successful, and profitable.

Let's imagine a corporate culture in which continuous improvement is a persistent state, with problem solving built into individual incentive plans and layered into the best practices of the firm.

I'm describing a culture geared toward excellence, one that proactively insulates a company from failure and optimizes the probability of success.

What company leader wouldn't jump at the chance to head up such a culture?

But how would a company operationalize such a cultural change?

Top management must encourage, allow, empower, and reward it, but top management cannot possibly know every problem, identify every inefficiency, and recognize every challenge. Thus, this must come from the stakeholders who have proximity and clarity around where and what problems exist. No doubt about this: Profitable Problem Solving and a culture of continuous improvement *must* include a grassroots campaign.

Grassroots? But can mid-level employees make that much of a difference? Absolutely.

> *"A body of determined spirits fired by an unquenchable faith in their mission can alter the course of history."*
> *- Mahatma Gandhi*

Grassroots movements have fueled social transformation for generations. Consider the civil rights movements, the suffrage movement, and the environmental movement. Were these not movements brought on by people coming together, despite much risk, to solve these disruptive and discriminatory issues?

> *"Never doubt that a small group of thoughtful, committed citizens can change the world. Indeed, it is the only thing that ever has."*
> *- Margaret Mead*

Imagine wholesale change in your company, beginning at the lowest levels. When everyone, from the entry level to the CEO, engages in problem solving, then the prospect of building a better organization becomes very real. When a company is able to keep employees and stakeholders focused on finding inefficiencies and issues and improving them, that company will operate on the basis of continuous improvement.

Imagine if General Motors CEO Mary Barra had a time machine. Long before she became CEO (in January 2014), as far back as 2004, reports indicate that GM had knowledge of a problem with an ignition switch placed in certain GM vehicles. Later reports from GM explained that when interrupted by a heavy key ring (yes, the weight of your key ring) or a jarring event, the ignition switch could slip out of the correct position and result in a power shutdown. The shutdown could then lead to a circumstance where the airbags could fail in a crash. Unfortunately, the sluggish problem-solving culture of the company was such that GM didn't begin recalling vehicles until 2014. Irresponsibly, they let that problem fester for a decade.

Sadly, the failures associated with the ignition switch not only resulted in a charge to earnings for GM of nearly $3 billion; it also was identified as a contributing factor in numerous traffic accidents that have cost many innocent victims their lives. Barra set up a victims' compensation fund that has approved 64 claims as of Q1 2015. GM estimates the fund will ultimately pay out over $600 million in claims.

Would GM and its customers have benefited from a culture in which employees were encouraged to identify problems and advance solutions when they were still small and manageable? You be the judge.

Not every company actively promotes a problem-solving culture, but I believe every company has within it employees imbued with the entrepreneurial spirit of creativity and problem-solving innovation. Americans in general, according to Gallop, are the most confident risk takers in the world.

Indeed, 96% of Americans believe themselves capable of accomplishing complicated and difficult endeavors, such as problem solving. Compare this to 91% of Chinese and 81% of citizens in the European Union.[1] It is true, most employees in the US fiercely believe themselves capable of solving problems. Since you are reading this book, I'll bet you're one of them.

Every existing company, including yours, would benefit from your efforts as a Profitable Problem Solver. Every CEO or other top manager would benefit from the value that Profitable Problem Solvers would bring to the company she leads. And as the company recognizes the benefit of your problem-solving efforts, you should be rewarded for tackling problems that would have otherwise handicapped the company's success down the road.

It would be a win-win situation for everyone, wouldn't it?

The opportunity is clear. When smart, creative, enthusiastic people are empowered and given incentive, they can learn to see the bigger picture, identify problems, and apply a new lens to inefficiencies in their own areas of responsibility. At the company level, this dynamic, innovative, problem-solving corporate culture is just waiting for the right champion to come along and introduce it.

So, what's stopping it from happening?

I have worked with many CEOs, CFOs, and COOs, in companies of all sizes, who tell me they are simply too busy to concern themselves with optimizing or remediating non-critical problems. Maintaining the status quo takes all their time and effort. Without realizing it, they have adopted an "if it ain't broke, don't fix it" attitude.

In those same businesses, I've met countless employees at every level who are painfully aware of problems within their organizations, have brilliant ideas on how to solve them, and yet feel they lack the support to suggest, let alone make, improvements.

As a result, nothing changes. Little problems grow into bigger issues.

Considering these two factors—leaders focused on the status quo and employees who don't feel empowered to suggest solutions—is it any surprise that so many businesses struggle and 25% of all small businesses fail in their first year?[2]

It doesn't get any prettier down the road. As the US Small Business Administration states, the failure rate increases to nearly 50% by the fifth year in business and increases again to 67% at the ten-year point. Sadly, the data indicate that only 25% of small businesses survive to their 15th anniversary. [3]

That statistic is sobering, but it is even more staggering when you consider how important small businesses are to our economy. To see the picture over a few decades, start looking historically back to 1982. Since then, the number of small businesses launched in the US has increased by 49%, and these small businesses have accounted for over eight million new jobs since 1990. [4]

This leads to an unassailable conclusion: Our economy needs successful entrepreneurs, and the organizations they build need talented employees who are able to identify bottlenecks, remediate problems, and optimize their surroundings.

This book was written as a wake-up call for those entrepreneurial problem solvers who desperately want to contribute to their organizations and—just as important—who want to be rewarded for their extraordinary performance. I also wrote it for CEOs who want to build their legacy by architecting corporate cultures characterized by creativity, innovation, and continuous improvement.

I have created some free tools for you to use with this book. Please visit www.profitableproblemsolving.com/freetools and download them today.

Chapter One

What Is Profitable Problem Solving?

The turning of the millennium—what doomsayers all around the globe called "Y2K"—was a time of fear, disruption, and distress across the entire span of industries. The large company for which I was working was no exception.

It was early in my career, and I was working in sales management. Every division of the company was struggling to maintain its sales targets, but I managed to find ways around the problems in my branch office. We kept meeting our targets, and before long, top management noticed my success.

They moved me to another branch within my region and told me, "Keep doing what you've been doing ..." A few months later, they moved me again, with the same mandate. "Do it again."

I was in heaven. To create a consistent recipe for success, I began to identify trends and collect data to track what I saw happening in the market. Based on those trends, I put together a strategic plan to navigate the difficult business environment. I proposed to provide this recipe to several high performers, send them out to struggling branches, have them replicate the success I had experienced thus far, and so create improvement across my division and drive real value for the company.

I'm sure my plan was far from perfect. It probably was not aligned exactly with the CEO's priorities, as I was still learning the nuances of how to drive growth. But my plan had all the essential ingredients: it identified challenges, provided data to illustrate the trends, suggested solutions, explained the costs, and clearly stated the value I expected to create when we declared the effort a success.

During a special visit from our division president, I presented my plan. She immediately recognized the possibilities in what I was proposing (by the way, she remains one of my valued mentors and a dear friend). She later promoted me to a position in which I was responsible for fixing one of the company's prized territories. This new role put me in close proximity to an exciting merger and gave me the opportunity to proactively solve issues associated with the integration of the new brand and service offerings, which would ultimately drive over $500M in revenue for the company.[5] Before long, I was being head-hunted to do the same for other companies.

Note what happened here.

By stepping outside of what I was required to do in my day-to-day job, I gave my company something of genuine value. Then, by giving the company a way to replicate and scale it, I made sure they were aware that my plan was about the company, not about me.

And yet, by approaching this problem-solving project in a selfless manner that appeared to target nothing but the best interests of the company, I created an almost direct connection to ways that I could profit from it. Win-Win.

That presentation became the fuel for what has, so far, been an incredible career. It turned me into someone with a reputation as a turnaround specialist. And, it became the seed of Profitable Problem Solving.

Motivation to Solve Problems

While conducting my doctoral research into people's motivation to solve problems, I interviewed many people at all levels in their organizations. Almost without fail, the individuals I interviewed told me they were aware of solvable problems confronting their organizations, felt they were capable of solving those problems, and truly wanted to solve them.

In some organizations, problems were solved swiftly and efficiently, and innovation happened all the time.

In other companies—not so much.

In fact, not at all.

So, what was the difference?

Why weren't all problems being solved at every level of their organizations?

Here's what I discovered. The individuals I interviewed expressed an almost universal sense that there would have been no reward in it for them, no incentive, not even recognition of their efforts—and thus, no spark to the problem-solving process. Not only that, they had the sense that their suggestions would have been unwelcome. Embedded in corporate cultures that seemingly had no interest in problem solving, these individuals full of potential, did their jobs, supported the status quo, kept their heads down, and watched their companies limp along.

The result?

These companies could have been running more efficiently, selling more products or services, gaining many more important customers, and—the bottom line—improving their profitability. Instead, systemic problems went unrecognized and unsolved, problems continued to erode profitability, and small problems often grew, over time, into major issues.

Are you ready to dig in? Yes? Great. In the pages ahead, I'm going to bring together two mindsets:

Geared for the top management team, how an organization can empower its people to identify and solve problems, and

Geared for entrepreneurial mindsets, how people within the organization can identify problems, solve them, and — an essential element of the process from the employee's perspective — get recognized as a problem solver and be rewarded for contributing to the organization's profitability.

What Type of Problems Can Profitable Problem Solving™ Solve, Anyway?

First, what kind of problems am I referring to? There doesn't exist a worker who would tell you, "My work environment is absolutely perfect, and there isn't a single problem I would like solved." We wouldn't be humans if we didn't wish for things to be at least a little bit better.

While researching for this book, I had the great pleasure to talk with hundreds of people about problems they encounter and the strategies they employ to solve them. During most focus group sessions, more than 50% of the people I interviewed would reference an issue they were having with a rude co-worker, a disingenuous supervisor, or a complicated compensation structure. All were certainly problems for that person, but they are not the type addressed in this book.

Profitable Problem Solving

When I say "profitable problem solving," I'm referring to a very specific approach to solving the profitability-eroding problems that exist in every company, at every level, and in every location.

In the simplest terms, Profitable Problem Solving is a set of actionable strategies that proactively protect the company from failure or proactively stop a problem from interfering with the company's success and get the problem solver credit for her efforts.

Because you are creating and initiating these strategies in a proactive manner, you may be able to solve the problem before it becomes critical. That is, when it is cheaper, easier, faster, and less painful.

Obviously, this is positive for the company—and it should also be positive for you, the entrepreneurial, successful problem solver.

Profitable Problem Solving is an incredibly flexible process, with applicability to myriad situations, industries, and levels of the organization.

Individuals of varying levels of experience, acumen, and capability can adapt it to their own situations.

Someone in a low-level administrative position or someone in a high-level executive role can use it effectively. Their concepts of reward and profit may be very different, but they can adopt these principles, formulate a problem-solving initiative, add value to their company, and benefit personally.

In this book, I intend to provide lots of wiggle space, a healthy dose of gray area, and plenty of nuance. After all, to make a program work within an established culture, it must be flexible and easy to adapt.

I hope to get the CEO, the entry-level employee, and everybody in between excited about identifying and solving problems in their own organizations and building a systematic approach to continuous improvement.

I encourage readers to pay close attention to these principles, apply them to their own situations, make them their own, and profit from them—and do that over, and over, and over.

In the next several chapters, I'm going to present guidelines for a six-step plan to strategically solve problems. Following this, I'll lay out a strategy to make sure solving corporate problems is a profitable endeavor for you.

The six steps are easy to remember. Just keep in mind the simple acronym P-R-O-F-I-T.

Problem Statement – Looking For Trouble

Research Trends – Build your Case

Outline Solution – Planning for Success

Forecast Cost – Be Smart with Resources

Identify Value – Use Factor 10 to Scale Value

Take Action – Execute with Confidence

CASE STUDY:
The Use of Case Studies in Profitable Problem Solving™

Profitable Problem Solving can be an important part of your future. To help you see the impact of utilizing the problem-solving and personal-branding strategies outlined in the following pages, I will share a case study after each chapter to help you see the principle play out in real life.

The case studies are exciting, contemporary examples of business-world rock stars—as well as catastrophic failures. You will read about McDonald's, General Motors, and Domino's Pizza. To dig into the mind of executives who have made their mark on the business world by empowering problem solvers, I will introduce you, up close and personal, to Jack Welch, John Chen, and Patrick Doyle. Most important, I'll introduce you to rock stars like Adam Kutac and Nellie Greely, who are making their mark in their companies and in their careers by employing Profitable Problem Solving in their daily pursuit of excellence.

Don't skip the case studies; they are an important part of the learning process.

Chapter Two

Problem Solving 101

Introduction to Problem Solving

American business is littered with the wreckage of companies that would have benefitted from Profitable Problem Solving.

Let's take a look at two.

Consider Blockbuster. Do you remember them? Maybe you remember the late fees?

So what happened? How did such a solid company fail? The answer is much more common than you would think. The market conditions and customer demand in which they functioned underwent rapid, profound change. Everyone knew that was happening. But top management within Blockbuster failed to grasp the nature of that change. And with that miss, they failed to innovate and evolve.

Clearly, the first big misstep for the leadership of Blockbuster was incorrectly categorizing themselves as a distributor for entertainment companies. Had they stuck to the business model put forth by entrepreneur David Cook, who founded the outfit in 1985, they might have understood that their differentiation was in their ability to out-retail their competitors and provide superior customer service by optimizing inventory and helping customers understand their options.

Instead, they became paralyzed with tunnel vision; their misconception was that their real mission was to be a glorified distribution model for Hollywood films.

Sure, in the early years, Blockbuster soared past the competition by providing real-time information about what was available to rent and, of those movies available to rent, what was interesting based on customer preference. Today, this isn't rocket science, but during Blockbuster's heyday, this was an innovative answer to an underserved market made up mostly of families interested in grabbing a great movie and having a superior customer experience.

Hollywood box office receipts were faltering, but that didn't change consumers' need for something to do with the time they would have spent watching movies (Blockbuster should have treated this as an opportunity).

Surely someone at Blockbuster understood that trends were changing, early on when the challenges were still simple, small, and mild. Someone at Blockbuster must have realized they had to adjust their business model and start making films available online. But Blockbuster's top management, possibly blinded by the previous phenomenal success of the company, failed to empower its employees to identify and solve the onrushing problems.

Obviously, the data and the looming trends were available to analyze, and someone was prepared to take advantage of them.

And someone did.

The proof? Netflix.

The fact that Netflix was in operation for six years before Blockbuster finally tried to adjust tells most business students that Blockbuster suffered from a failure of management, rather than falling victim to changing market factors.[6]

Or how about our second big loser example, Kodak, employer of 140,000 people, market valued at $28 billion, and the king of film photography? But Kodak's phenomenal success with film and its rigid commitment to that medium prevented the company from pivoting toward the new world of digital photography. If you tell me no one at Kodak saw the digital-photography tsunami on the horizon, well, I simply won't believe it. It was a problem with a solution, but the Kodak corporate culture was unprepared to respond. So in 2012, the same year Kodak was filing bankruptcy, Instagram was busy counting the more than 100 million users subscribing to their service and planning for their acquisition by Facebook for $1B in cash and stock. There was definitely a market for Kodak to continue to lead; unfortunately, the management team failed to look beyond their "status quo" mentality and let Instagram run away with their market share.[7]

Entrepreneurial problem solvers within Blockbuster and Kodak, empowered by top management, surely could have suggested process innovation or product changes that would have addressed—that could have *solved*—these problems before they became fatal.

Again, the point is to solve these problems before a fatal blow is dealt. It means you are not hunting elephants; rather, you are looking for the smaller issues that have not yet evolved into an enterprise-threatening crisis. Indeed, in this stage, most of these issues seem everyday and simple.

Here are a few of the forms they can take:

Customer satisfaction issues that result in lost sales.

Poorly designed customer service centers that fail to satisfy customer expectations when attempting to resolve an issue with their products or service;

Inadequate ecommerce systems that make purchasing a product or service cumbersome, time consuming, or confusing; and

Customer service representatives not properly empowered to solve a customer issue during the reporting of the problem.

Inefficient processes that result in lost time and money.

Inventory management that results in waste or loss;

Poor management of resources that results in idle assets; and

Waste of fuel, water, and energy.

Cultural issues that result in workforce turnover and attrition.

Lack of HR diversity programs;

Poorly designed compensation plans and lack of fair wages; and

A culture that breeds ambiguity or poor employee satisfaction.

Liquidity challenges that require abrupt cost cutting.

Lack of sufficient capital to launch;

Supplier issues and escalations; and

Lack of profitability.

Product failures that result in customer complaints and lost profits.

Variation in production that results in poor product performance;

Failure to provide features and amenities expected by customer segment; and

Overselling expectations that result in customer disappointment with product.

This is just a small sampling of issues that seem manageable today, but when left unresolved, can prevent the company from operating at its highest possible efficiency, unnecessarily increase costs, reduce sales, and obstruct the company from achieving its greatest possible profits—or or even, in the most extreme circumstances, from surviving.

Whose Job Is Solving Problems? *Everyone's!*

Among other functions, top management of any organization is tasked with identifying and solving the problems that could handicap the company from achieving its highest possible profitability.

Some of the simplest problems may be apparent to the CEO, especially in a small to midsize company, and she may be able to introduce a top-down solution. However, no CEO is ever in a position to truly observe every day-to-day operation. She is likely unable to see problems that may be obvious to employees at different levels in the organization, in different offices, in different locations. If these employees were empowered to identify and solve problems, wouldn't this create a corporate culture worthy of the most efficient, most profitable company possible?

Isn't this the sort of company the CEO would want to lead?

And, if you are an ambitious, creative, entrepreneurial member of the team, isn't this the kind of company you want to work for?

Classify the Obvious to Build Understanding

As a society, we are accustomed to seeing universal issues classified by their different stages. Certainly, you have heard people talk about the stages of grief, stages of sleep, and stages of change.

Here is an oldie but goodie. You may or may not remember the Bruce Tuckman model of group development, but you likely remember the stages he introduced to explain group dynamics: Forming, Storming, Norming, and Performing.

Since we all likely agree that problem-solving behavior is ubiquitous, doesn't it make sense to classify the types of problems and provide stages of problem solving? If we are still in agreement, we're in luck: that is exactly where this story will take us.

After high school, I joined the Army Reserve to help pay my way through college. Today's new recruits may have a different experience, but when I enlisted, it was a fast and rather simple process. Basically, you went to the recruiter's office, looked over a few pamphlets depicting soldiers in various military jobs (infantry, logistics, police, operations, etc.), and selected the career that appealed to you. The recruiter determined if you scored high enough on your *Armed Services Vocational Aptitude Battery (ASVAB)*, and you were on your way. Literally, on your way to boot camp.

As quickly as I pointed to a picture of soldiers decontaminating armored vehicles from dangerous chemicals,

I was heading off to train for my new career as a Nuclear, Biological, Chemical Warfare Specialist—more often referred to in military circles at that time as 54 Bravo.

One of the first things my new military colleagues and I learned was MOPP. That is an acronym for Mission Oriented Protective Posture. It's a simple way to remember the classification of biological and chemical threats and the corresponding level of readiness to ensure survival (yes— survival). Definitely important stuff!

Depending on the threat level of chemical or biological hazards, soldiers go into ever-higher MOPP levels.

MOPP Ready: Protective mask is carried. First set of suit, gloves, and boots are available within two hours, second set within six hours.

MOPP Level 0: Protective mask carried. Suit, gloves, and boots accessible/available.

MOPP Level 1: Suit worn. Mask, gloves, and boots carried.

MOPP Level 2: Suit and boots worn. Gloves and mask carried.

MOPP Level 3: Suit, boots, and mask worn. Gloves carried.

MOPP Level 4: All protection worn.[8]

Here is the thing: without the categories, we would not have known how to prepare quickly. If we were unprepared and in a real wartime environment with hazardous chemicals or biological contaminants, the impact could be devastating.

Categories help us quickly understand exactly what we need to do.

The categories in the Profitable Problem Solving Roadmap™ will help you know just what to do—or not do—when when solving problems.

<u>Chapter Three</u>

Problem Solving 101 (Part I)

The Profitable Problem Solving Roadmap™

The Profitable Problem Solving Roadmap™ looks like a beast upon first glance … but if we break it down, I think you'll see that this can be your quick and easy go-to tool to determine what and when to solve.

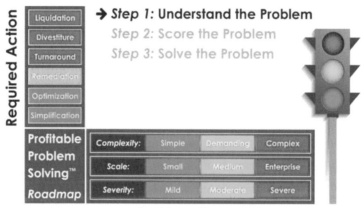

Problem Prognosis

    I bet you are already a step ahead of me and have realized the roadmap is set up in a graph format. Graphs are a great tool to impart understanding when data, relationships, and correlations are involved.

    Maybe it has been a while, so here is a quick reminder from your ninth-grade math class to make sure you remember how to use the X and the Y axes to follow the plotted course. Here is a fun visual mnemonic device:

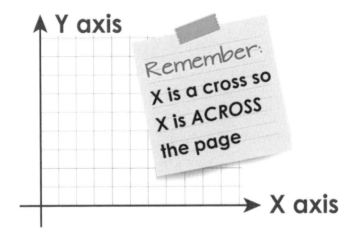

So ... let's get started by getting familiar with the Profitable Problem Solving Matrix by heading up the Y axis.

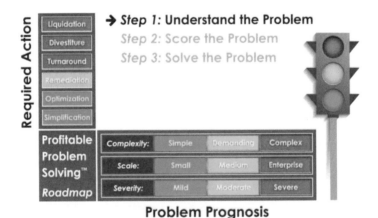

Simplification

This type of problem-solving activity is all about removing the complexity from a task, a process, or an interaction.

Picture yourself in an airport ticket line or a line for tickets at a theater. You're in luck! There's almost no one in line ahead of you. But between you and the ticket agent, there's a maze of posts-and-ropes. The ticket counter is 10 feet away as the crow flies, but it's going to take you 50 yards of back-and-forth to reach it. As you turn each little corner, you wonder aloud: *Why am I doing this?* Sure, some people are brave enough to unhook the security lane and walk right through, but most people just follow the path—even though it's obviously a pointless exercise.

The simplification of a complex task can be very valuable to a company. In N. Gopalakrishnan's book *Simplified Lean Manufacture,* we learn about a chemical plant in Dubai that observed one operator walking 480 meters (for those of us who grew up in the US, that is a nearly a third of a mile) to deliver chemicals needed to complete a work order. To their surprise, this same operator was making this trip ten times a day to complete the number of work orders he was required to close. In the end, the plant estimated that this operator walked 4.8 kilometers (almost a full three miles).

Are you shocked by this example? What if this operator had sought to simplify the task and requested that his work station be closer to the chemical supply, or if a daily amount of chemical stock could be supplied to his work station, thus negating his need to walk back and forth so much, so often?

Look around you. Simplification can happen in so many different ways. Here are a few simple ones you can probably spot in your first search:

Example 1:

What about the delivery driver who successfully simplifies her route to remove unnecessary stops or departures? This simple initiative will result in saving time and fuel. Another possible benefit to the company, the driver can use the extra time to add more stops to the route and improve her daily productivity.

Example 2:

How many hours do you think you waste sitting in or hosting meetings that are not working (as I used to say on the sales floor) closest to the dollar? In other words, are you sitting in 90-minute calls that really shouldn't take more than 30 minutes? The dreaded "Status Update" calls are often big offenders, stealing productive time from high-performing employees. Consider revisiting the agenda to make sure the right people are in the right meeting and their time isn't wasted. This can increase productivity and employee satisfaction. Often, status updates can be done in a status report form during less peak hours and made available to leadership in a shared drive that everyone can access if the information is helpful to others. While this doesn't remove the benefit of a status call, it does give the host of the call a chance to remove the everyday, unchanged updates for projects in process and invite each member of the team to share only new, critical updates, thus reducing the amount of time in the update meeting.

Example 3:

The US Travel Association reports that US residents logged 452 million trips for business purposes in 2013. Those are big numbers. When you look at the impact to business, companies spend over \$260 billion on travel and count 2.3 million jobs impacted by travel. Imagine the opportunities to simplify and save by adjusting a travel requirement in favor of an Internet-based collaboration tool. This could reduce the cost and hardship of travel and contribute to the work/life balance of employees who would otherwise have to travel. The same study by the US

Travel Association indicated that businesses take in an average of $9.50 of increased revenue and $2.90 in new profits from every dollar invested in business travel. Take that into perspective and think about how to simplify the process to obtain the same average results, while still easing the total number of trips a year.

Now you likely see that simplification is something that everyone can do in her job. There are more challenging examples of simplification. For example, one of my executive coaching clients sought to simplify the customer service center of the company he worked for. This client was a real go-getter, climbing the ladder at a fast pace and loving it. In efforts to improve the net promoter score of the midsize Internet-services firm he worked for, he devised a plan right out of a Jim Champy book which focused on reducing complexity and increasing customer satisfaction. His plan was brilliant, based on trends that he observed: customers were unable to get a solution to a problem with their customer service reps in one touch (in other words, before the client was transferred to another customer service rep in a supervisory position). He sought to simplify the steps needed to solve the top 20 typical issues for which customers called the service center. In other words, Tom would make it easier for the customer service reps to solve the most common problems in one step, instead of many. Tom estimated that 80% of the top 20 complaints were delivery issues, product issues, general complaints, or billing issues. Management approved this project, implemented it over a three-month period, and then hailed it as a huge success as the company observed a significant improvement in customer service satisfaction and net promoter score. The value of Tom's solution? Over \$4M in the first 24 months.

The key takeaway is that simplification projects are the best place for you to start, especially if you are new to profitable problem solving. In Chapter 10, I'll discuss how to scale the value of the solution with Factor 10, so management will understand your solution's true value and how to build a portfolio of solved problems that lead you to personal gain and improved personal wealth.

Optimization

Optimization has some characteristics that make it more challenging than simplification. Optimization may involve reducing complexity, but not necessarily. Optimization is the act or the methodology responsible for making a task, process, or event as perfect as possible. Perfection is somewhat relative here, as the optimized state of some process does not mean the sky is the limit for the results of any optimized task or process; rather, it means the company reengineers the process to function in a manner that delivers the optimal results, given the constraints the process contains.

Consider any key task or process. You, the problem-solving guru in training, will likely see a chance to optimize the world in which you work. While optimization is not as basic as simplification, it is often easier to gain support for optimization options, as the process or tasks are likely already part of your company's best practices.

Let's explore some examples of optimization:

Profit optimization—A clear favorite of shareholders and investors. Your optimization can seek to perfect the profitability of a product or service offering, a profit center, or an entire company. Profits are increased when more dollars drop to the bottom line. The usual levers to increase profits include an increase in revenue, decrease in cost, or improvement in efficiency (that can improve time to value). While this is an exceptionally high level, it is intended to help you see where and how you might begin your search for opportunities to optimize profitability for your company.

Sales optimization—The sales process can often grow into a set of complicated interactions with a customer that result in too many opportunities for the prospect to lose interest or reconsider her desire to buy. As I learned early in my career, *time kills all deals.* The most effective sales environments nurture a swift, smart, value-oriented connection with prospects. The more Joe on the sales floor has to call the prospect to get a *Yes*, the higher the statistical probability that the prospect will drop out of the process. What is a sales leader to do? It is rare that a salesperson can quickly pass by gatekeepers and connect with the right buyer in the customer's organization, qualify their needs, introduce them to the right product or service, overcome the prospect's objections, and close the optimal deal structure in one call. Even if you have a product or service that lends itself to a one-call close, you still run into prospects who want to "think about it," "explore other options," or "check all your company's references." These are important steps to the buyer, yet they result in extra time in the sales process. Smart sales leaders build a sales process that trains and supports salespeople at every stage of the deal (prospecting, active sales, and delivery), in a manner designed with the highest probability of closing the deal. These smart sales leaders arm themselves with customer relationship management (CRM), business intelligence (BI), and social sales solutions to identify and track progress with target prospects. These products help the sales leaders on the floor track everything from the most granular amount of total dials to slicing the type of connections into a dashboard of sales productivity metrics.

Let's peek in on a real-world example that fits a long list of mid- to Fortune 100-size service organizations. Our real-world example company, ABC Services, has a go-to market strategy that relies on what a salesperson would call *a three-call close*. In other words, the ABC prescriptive sales process predicts a salesperson working hard to sell the deal should close in three calls—not four, not five. Of course, the salesperson isn't lucky enough to start with a list of prospects already qualified and ready to go—*nope*—she has to whittle down a list of 100 cold call dials a day to make a living on a three-call close product. Here are some of the metrics ABC would study and seek to optimize on the sales floor:

Opportunity Rate—The percent of time a salesperson can get the actual decision maker on the phone (thus getting past the gatekeepers and avoiding the dreaded transfer to voicemail).

Set Rate—The percent of time a salesperson sets a demo or final proposal call.

Hold Rate—The percent of time the salesperson's demo or final proposal calls are successfully delivered. In other words, does the salesperson develop true interest in her prospects, or is she setting closing appointments that are not likely to really happen?

Closing—the almighty metric that compares the percent of deals closed to total deals attempted.

So here is the thing. Over time, ABC had designed a sales process to combat every objection a prospect might have and increase the opportunity for a salesperson to communicate the value of ABC's services. In efforts to give the salespeople the best path to a *yes*, they added multiple steps in the sales process, provided scripts that made the sales calls too long, and insisted on a complicated discount program that left the salesperson rushing to explain how the savings worked before the prospect hung up the phone.

ABC could optimize the process by reducing the complexity and moving to a two-call close. The reduction in time in the buying process would result in higher sales and profit margins for ABC.

Optimizing a sales process is not often as simple as the ABC suggestion implies, but it is definitely something that can provide some quick, valuable results. If you are in sales, I can almost guarantee you can find a part of the sales process to optimize.

Remediation

Remediation is very different from simplification and optimization in that remediation is about fixing a problem or defect that exists (unlike simplification and optimization, where you are making something acceptable better). Remediation is the process of creating a remedy or fix to a problem—that is left in a problem state—that results in some type of loss or risk for the company.

Here's a true story. I purchased a *"big deal"* from Angie's List. If you are unfamiliar, Angie's List is a cool service that helps consumers find qualified professionals from a community of buyers who have provided references. They call their specials offered by qualified vendors "big deals."

This particular big deal was a special for a painter to paint three rooms for a special, all-inclusive price. After talking with the painter who offered the deal and letting him know what type of paint I wanted in each room, I was surprised to hear that he didn't want to do the work, as he didn't want to deal with latex paint on the wood trim. He suggested I call Angie's List and get a refund. So, as you might guess, my next call was to their customer service center.

I was informed that I could not get a refund; however, I could have the several hundred dollars I had paid for the special as a credit on my account for some other offering that I might want in the future. Well, no one likes being told they can't receive a refund, but I decided to get over my frustration and put the credit toward something else I needed to buy. Sure enough, a situation presented itself a few weeks later when my daughter was moving from one apartment to another and was struggling to make the time in her busy EMT schedule (lots of 24-hour shifts) to complete the move. It was clear she was working hard to differentiate herself in her new profession. I was determined to help. I looked on Angie's List and found a "big deal" in her new zip code for moving services. The new "big deal" was $11.00 more than the credit I had on my Angie's List account. I called their customer service center once again to apply the credit. I won't take you through the entire call, but here are the highlights:

Sorry, Ma'am, we will have to change your address in the system to make it seem you live in the new zip code so you can purchase a big deal in a different city than the one you have on file in your account.

Sorry, Ma'am, we can't just bill your credit card for the $11.00; you will have to (again) pay the entire amount of $310.00, and then we will credit the $299.00 you have as a credit back to your credit card in the form of a refund.

By the way, Ma'am, looks like your account is coming up for renewal, would you like to renew into an upgraded account?

Really? I'm not happy and you want to sell me something else? I bet you can say this with me, "How about you just transfer me to a supervisor?" And with that, the polite, but less than helpful, customer service representative transferred me to a supervisor in their big deal department. I must admit, I was not expecting much better from the second call. And yet, one of the most talented customer service reps I have ever encountered took my call and changed the course of events. The supervisor came on the call quickly and introduced herself as Kelly. She admitted that employees are challenged to deal with the systems, too (validating my frustration), and that their systems were in the process of going through some upgrades that would improve their credit and escalation system in the next six to twelve months (giving me hope things will be better soon). Kelly assured me that she could handle the entire process on her end and would call me back with final details of the purchase and refund.

I stopped her at this point and said that while she was definitely making the process less disruptive for me, I was still disappointed with the lengthy process I had to experience and the fact that I was unable to get a refund in the first place. I told her that if I were able to review Angie's List as I can the vendors in their network, this would be a negative review.

Again, Kelly's skills were superb. Without any pause or animosity, she told me that I absolutely could review Angie's List and that the company would appreciate the constructive feedback. She promised to send me an email with the details of how to leave a public review for Angie's List on their system. Further, she offered to provide me with a renewal for the following year membership for no charge as an apology (gave me something for my trouble) and, just like that, I was a happy Angie's List customer.

Clearly, from the message to customers, Angie's List is remediating systems and process—and with good reason. Another important aspect, the remediation was clearly communicated within the company, as I was able to discern that the supervisor dealing with customer escalations was relying on the corrections to the process and technology to result in enhanced functionality that would make satisfying customer requests an easier, happier experience. Kelly's great customer service—and the knowledge that Angie's List seems to be looking for innovative ways to improve—will likely keep me a customer of Angie's List for a long time.

Remediation can take place in almost any critical function of the company. Consider within your own firm how many times you may have heard about improvement initiatives coming from information technology (IT), finance and accounting (F&A), governance, risk, and compliance (GRC), and supply chain (SC).

Turnaround

I love turnaround discussions, as this is where I have hit most of my homeruns. The idea that a company or division has so many critical failures impacting brand, sales, liquidity, and profitability all at once is much like the business version of a decathlon. Because the ten track-and-field events in the decathlon are so grueling and require such an adaptive, diverse athlete, the winner of the Olympic decathlon has historically claimed the title of the *world's greatest athlete*. This is a title they truly deserve after winning in such a broad and complex environment.

Let me just say, the turnaround is a problem you need a specialist to solve. You likely wouldn't operate on a patient if you were not a surgeon, fly a plane if you are not a pilot, or dive off the top of a skyscraper if you were not an experienced (and adrenaline-crazed) base jumper. The point here: the problem is complicated and has tremendous consequences if not done quickly and done right. Remember, the company is experiencing multiple failures at once.

You might look at the Profitable Problem Solving matrix and say, "Hey, it looks as if you can have a turnaround that registers in the simple range of complexity, small in scale, and mild in severity (I know we are jumping ahead, but work with me for a second). I would say that is highly unlikely. There are some exceptions to every rule, but in the turnaround world, it is not statistically probable. You might have a sole-proprietorship that is failing in several areas, and the entrepreneur can bring stabilization to the company by infusing cash and resources; but beyond the sole-proprietorship or micro-business models, my suggestion is to leave the turnaround to the experienced turnaround specialist. If this type of work appeals to you, consider this when you begin to build your portfolio of problem-solving accomplishments and grow your skillset. I am proof (along with a couple of American Business Awards that I shamelessly mention here) that becoming a turnaround specialist is a goal that can be achieved with the right dedication and commitment.

If I have not yet belabored the need for a turnaround specialist, I will soon. Later in this book, you will read case studies about John Chen, Tony Hsieh, and Jack Welch. All three are absolute CEO rock stars in the world of business. The case studies will detail their specific actions. In this chapter, let's look at what they had in common.

A turnaround has many issues, but only a few goals. While companies fail for various reasons, the goals of turnarounds are surprisingly similar. A turnaround must (1) diagnose the failure points resulting in the immediate failure(s); (2) introduce a multi-dimensional plan to stop the bleeding and find a source of short-term profitability to sustain the firm through the transformation process; and (3) bring forth wholesale transformation that restores the path to long-term profitability. The how, what, when, and why of these oversimplified goals are unique to each turnaround.

When I look over my career, I have a hard time picking favorites from my accomplishments. But I must confess, the turnaround of America's SAP Users' Group (ASUG) is definitely on my shortlist.

In early 2009, a recruiter reached out to me after hearing about some of my turnaround and business improvement accomplishments in the software services industry. He mentioned that ASUG was looking for an interim CEO to drive the organization through stabilization and rebuilding strategy. He knew I had a rich history with SAP and a great track record when it came to making good stories out of potential failures. By June, I was accepting the role of interim CEO and digging into the details. It did not take long to realize that we were in big trouble. While the company did have some strategic reserves set aside for a rainy day, without drastic changes and an infusion of cash, it looked like the company would soon be running out of operating cash. We were two months from missing payroll.

Almost overnight, I built an incredible team, leveraged an experienced board of directors, and set out on a 100-day plan to restore liquidity and stability. The 100-day plan was a success.

From there, ASUG focused on a plan to transform the company in 24 months. We reached our goal in 18 months with better results than we had expected. The transformation insulated the company from future liquidity crises, we got all the hair out of the operations, and we built a culture that was focused on doing more for the company and customers.

By the end of my five years with ASUG, our transformation had moved into the continuous improvement phase of our plan and was trending up on all indicators of long-term profitability. Over those five years, we took home some cool awards for executive and company success. Today, ASUG is able to represent more than 80% of the SAP North American customer base and over 10% of the global customer base. This is a testament to the turnaround, the board of directors, and the current CEO and team that continue to steer the ship in the right direction.

Divestiture

A divestiture, essentially, is the full or partial removal of a department, division, line of business, partnership, or subsidiary. The divestiture (or removal) can be accomplished in a couple different ways, including selling the unit, liquidation, or bankruptcy. Like a turnaround, divestiture requires specialists, from strategy building through to project completion.

As you will see later in this book when we dig into the accomplishments of Jack Welch, a divestiture is not necessarily a bad thing. A divestiture can take place because the unit is not considered core to the parent company's model or it is not operating in a manner that satisfies the original mission.

One of my clients, Meg, was driving an incredibly successful start-up that was boasting crazy growth figures in the first 18 months from launch. As you may know, when a start-up experiences extraordinary growth, they may experience significant disruption if they are not well capitalized in the beginning of their entrepreneurial endeavor. In fact, this is the death spiral for many start-ups. They grow much faster than the business can generate cash, and without some investment, they end up failing to deliver to clients, pay suppliers, or pay employees (maybe all three).

The Kardashian business isn't the only one built on drama. Every company has some drama, and Meg's organization was no exception. When Meg and her co-founding partner conceived of the new entrepreneurial endeavor, they decided to combine forces to make one great company. Meg was courting several large consulting contracts that would hit the ground running and require some cash, resources, and a back office to handle the billing and HR demands of the new contracts. Meg's co-founder was nearly ready to pull the trigger on a $10M acquisition of a staffing company focused on technology and engineering talent. The company Meg's partner was acquiring had an established back office, reliable HR process, and enough profitability to cover the needs Meg's consulting contracts would add to the picture if they merged their efforts. Just like that, a company was born. Meg would build a new, consultative, margin-rich offering on top of the existing staffing model that was generating dependable cash and revenues.

Are you able to guess what happened? Yep. Meg closed the contracts and brought on nearly $15M in business in just a couple of months, and her co-founder partner failed to deliver on the acquisition. Now Meg's new company was in trouble.

The co-founder partner tried diligently to build the back office from scratch, but she made so many mistakes along the way that the company was unable to understand the true cost of operations, forecast cash, or execute basic accounts receivable and accounts payable functions. The obvious solution: Get rid of the co-founder partner and the infrastructure the partner was building.

That is when I came on the scene. Because the outgoing stakeholder was a shareholder of considerable voting power, we had to divest the new entity of the emerging staffing model and all that went with it, which covered the three usual suspects: people, process, and technology.

The divestiture took some time due to these sensitive issues. When all was said and done, Meg was able to move into an array of remediation projects to get the back office (now free of confusion and flaws) up to the level required to support the existing business and scale to cover new business.

As for Meg's co-founder partner, the new staffing agency (created as a result of the divestiture) had a slow, but steady, start. The two firms negotiated a preferred supplier agreement so that Meg could source new talent for growing contract requirements from the staffing agency. A win-win for sure.

Liquidation

Liquidation doesn't sound good, does it?

It is not.

Liquidation is the usual alternative to bankruptcy. Just like turnaround and divestiture, experts handle liquidation. If the firm is of any material size, the experts usually include a cadre of lawyers. The experts, especially the legal teams, are needed because issues arising during liquidation can create liability and risk for those making key decisions. An agency problem, something to definitely avoid, happens when control agents (corporate decision makers) are expected to make decisions that benefit or protect a certain group, but are motivated by self-interest and thus may not operate or act in the best interest of the group they are charged to serve.

Not to get too technical here, but at some point during a liquidation, the firm's leadership will find themselves operating in what is technically referred to as the *zone of insolvency*. The courts differ on when a company actually enters the zone of insolvency, as it is sometimes hard to pinpoint where and when the financial struggle began. But from a practitioner's perspective, you can definitely tell when the company has arrived in the zone of insolvency because they are barely above water and sinking fast. There are tests used by the court to confirm the diagnosis; these include the Balance Sheet test and the Equity test. Based on my informal perspective, a company reaches the zone of insolvency when the company's book value is insufficient to cover near-term commitments.

It is important for a problem solver to identify this stage of failure, because the zone of insolvency brings with it a shift in duties for officers and control agents of the companies. Simply put, there are certain stages of failure that require the officers and control agents of the company to shift from a singular focus on shareholders to a dual focus on shareholders and creditors.

You can see how an agency problem might develop now, right? Most company officers and control agents are shareholders and employees themselves. With this shift in duties, there are now decisions that have to be made to protect creditors that might jeopardize the interests of employees or investors. Unfortunately, not every corporate officer makes the right decision, and some land in pretty significant legal trouble of their own. The alumni on this list are sadly numerous. It includes executives from the likes of Enron, Goldman Sachs, and WorldCom.

Chapter Four

Profitable Problem Solving 101 (Part II)

Complexity, Scale, Severity

Okay, now that we have familiarized ourselves with the different types of actions a problem solver might undertake (simplification, optimization, remediation, turnaround, divestiture, and liquidation), let's switch gears and examine the parameters of every problem-solving initiative — *complexity, scale,* and *severity* — and examine how those terms fit into the Profitable Problem Solving Roadmap.

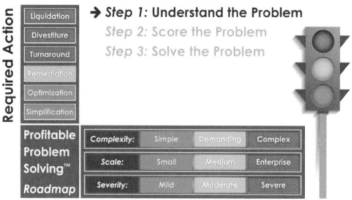

Problem Prognosis

Across the X axis, there are three dimensions of problem characteristics that you should understand as you embark on your problem-solving crusade.

Complexity:

Whether the issue is professional or personal, complexity is a fact of life. Everyone loves to complicate matters that could (and should) stay simple.

Why is that? Do people complicate things in order to showcase their intellect, or do they complicate iteratively without realizing they are adding to the problem? My research suggests that there is a fair amount of both.

For our Profitable Problem Solving purposes, you need to know only this: *Complex does not always equal smart.* In fact, in my experience, it rarely does. The simplest solution, the one involving the fewest steps and the fewest people, is often—*is almost always*—the one with the highest probability of success.

If we agree that you can be smart by demystifying rather than complicating, then you can see why understanding the complexity of a problem is a key part to solving it.

The problem-solving road map illustrates the three degrees of complexity: simple, demanding, and complex.

Simple

Your problem belongs in the "simple" category if it is a singular task, process, or activity that can be isolated and simplified. If you take a 360-degree look at your job and all you must do in a day to be successful, you will likely find many issues that are simple in nature and easy to correct.

Example:

To save time and increase productivity, you plan to shorten the amount of distance between your workstation and the tools you need to complete a task.

Demanding

Instead of simple, utilize the "demanding" category if your problem includes an array of tasks, processes, or activities that relate to one another.

Example:

To increase customer satisfaction and attract new customers, a dry cleaner introduced curbside service. This service solved the daily problems experienced by counter staff during peak hours to get customers in and out of the store in a quick and happy manner. To solve this problem, the owner had to focus on the handful of tasks, all related to the intake and the return of clothes to customers, and optimize those activities to fit the new curbside model.

Complex

And last but not least, use the complex category when you face a problem-solving project that includes many unrelated tasks, processes, or activities. Often, the complexity is generated by the need to employ parallel processing (fixing multiple issues at once) to deal with a complex problem. Some project managers who are responsible for complex projects that include parallel processing describe themselves as the air traffic controller of the solution, since there are so many moving pieces.

Example:

To improve the outlook for long-term profitability, the owner of a consulting agency announced to her company that she was launching a brand transformation initiative. In order to mature the brand and attract higher-margin customers, the owner had to refine the value proposition and the way the company differentiated on the web, in marketing materials, and in sales calls. To accomplish this goal, the marketing team, web development team, sales team, technical sales advisors, project managers, and consultants had to reimagine the manner in which they messaged value, sold their services, delivered their services, and sought testimonials and case studies from successful project experiences. This complex problem took nearly six months, required parallel processing of activities, and affected the entire company. Once the project was complete, the company had to move into an intensive training phase to learn how to use the new tools and messaging to the company's advantage.

Okay, so we've figured out dimension one, *Complexity*. It's not so difficult to imagine how to utilize this dimension in categorizing your future problem-solving initiatives.

Let's keep moving to the second dimension: *Scale*. Scale is no more difficult than complexity to apply.

Scale

The big question for us at this juncture is: *How big is the issue?* Do you need to call in the cavalry? Or rather, is this something that you (or you and a small team) can tackle? To better identify the right scale, ask yourself how many departments are impacted by the problem. How many fellow employees will be disrupted by the solution? What resources are required to implement a solution? Are the solutions within your own arm's reach?

Small

Solving small problems can be relatively easy, highly valuable to the organization, and very profitable to you. I say "easy" because you are capable of solving the problem without engaging any other problem solvers. Yes, this is a problem you can successfully solve on your own.

Sidebar for a moment: I have observed highly capable people opting to pass by the chance to solve a smaller, simpler problem (and thus leave it unsolved and incubating for the later day when it is more complex and expensive to solve) for a more seemingly complicated and "value-oriented" problem. Remember this, folks ... just because a problem is small does not mean that it will yield small value. When you extrapolate the value across your department, division, company, or industry, you may be looking at some substantial figures for savings or growth. In later chapters, I will dive into the language of value and teach you how to use a proxy for forecasting the value of your problem-solving effort across the organization. I call it *Factor 10 Value* (and I'll discuss it at length in Chapter 10).

Example:

A project manager has experienced some recent, unexpected delays associated with her team of programmers, and as a result, she is late on delivering the final code for an important milestone in the project plan. If she has another delay, the project will go over the approved budget. To improve her ability to proactively impact on-time/on-budget activities, the project manager makes changes to the format her team of developers use to report their daily accomplishments. She also requires them to report their updates every day. As a result of asking the right questions more often, she is armed with more opportunities to help lead her team to a successful project.

Medium

As we move to the middle of the spectrum, you will find problems that require more than one person to solve. To classify your problem scale as medium, the team of problem solvers must all be related to one another by either their chain of command, working within the same department or division, or being allocated to the same project.

A medium problem-solving effort is likely to be chartered by a director or vice president who has some type of ownership or responsibility for the cost center to which the team is charged in the annual budget. Why? Simply put, when you add requirements or redirect personnel within a company, you are asking them to spend less time on something else. While most employees are accustomed to being asked to do more with less, it's likely that when a new project is kicked off, something else that previously had the team's attention will be handled much slower or stalled altogether until your project is complete. The best way to avoid issues in a political, corporate environment with many dotted lines to leadership is to proactively communicate the time and impact of your project to those who could disrupt your efforts down the road.

By building an informal team, you may run a smaller risk of disrupting existing workloads. What is the difference between a formal team and an informal team? In a word, *power*. Power refers to the type of leadership applied to a scenario to achieve a desired goal.

If your power comes from your *authority,* then you will likely be more formal and direct about assigning requirements and holding the team accountable.

If, however, your power comes from the *influence* you can productively assert, then you may be more likely to build informal teams of people who commit to helping you accomplish your goals due to your leadership style, charisma, or the fact that you share a common cause or purpose. In this manner, you may identify a problem that can be solved by teaming together with a few peers who share the same problem. The good news is that your leadership is in the DNA of the project, since it came from your perspective, and you can still take significant credit for accomplishments of the group. When we dig into how a problem solver can use Factor 10 to scale the value of a project, we will also dive into the specific area of value we call *Factor 10 Reach.* Factor 10 Reach will help guide you to productive strategies for creating personal gain for the solutions you accomplish.

For now, let's stay focused on scale. Remember, it doesn't matter if you lead a team in a formal or informal manner. It just matters that you have the right people on your team and everyone understands the goals and path to success.

Example:

A shop foreman has just been informed that his VP has denied his request for new equipment; moreover, he needs to build in a five percent improvement to the Manufacturing Cycle Time (MCT measures the time is takes to produce a product from order to finished goods) metric for his plant. Determined to turn this problem into an opportunity, the shop foreman assembles a meeting with the plant managers who run each shift and explains in a positive manner that another year will pass before the new equipment will be on the floor, but they can make some improvements along the way that will allow them to safely and productively use the existing equipment and still improve the MCT. He asks the managers to build a list of the top five issues that slow down the manufacturing process, and then they devise a plan to solve those top three issues. The team totally buys into the plan, even though this is not an officially sanctioned project from corporate. The team decides they can reduce the waiting time by clarifying orders before they get to the shop, reduce bottlenecks by changing the number of employees on the line, and switch from a local freight company to UPS (whose shipments are trackable and guaranteed). After just one fiscal quarter of the team working to optimize these three issues, the shop foreman receives an excited call from the VP, who has noticed that MCT is improving much faster than they had expected, which provides just enough justification to approve the new equipment. A win-win deal.

Enterprise

Enterprise-wide issues impact the entire company in one way or another. To categorize the scale of a problem-solving effort as enterprise-wide, the coordination of the teams needs to come from a strategic, top level of management.

Why would this type of issue require such a strategic project champion? If an issue requires management to delegate tasks across multiple shifts, departments, divisions, or subsidiaries, you will find that accountability will only be effective if it rests with a few leaders at the top who can exert power, via both authority and influence, across different cost, profit, and technical silos. The titles that you might expect to see leading enterprise-scale projects include general manager, vice president, president, owner, chief operating officer, chief information officer, chief financial officer, chief marketing officer, or chief executive officer. Note that this list isn't exhaustive and isn't necessarily true for every company.

Example:

The CEO has asked the COO to lead the company's new focus on sustainability. The COO's knowledge about sustainability is not sufficient to build the enterprise-wide implementation plan. To make sure the company has the best plan, the COO hires a highly regarded expert on sustainability in their industry. The expert works at a strategic level with the COO in building plans, budgets, risk analysis, and an executive dashboard to track the success and value of the initiative. The expert also works with the hands-on VPs and directors who have been identified by the COO as having specific responsibility for leading their teams toward sustainability achievements. After 18 months of hard work, nearly every department in the company, having completed their required project tasks, is operating in a more sustainable manner. To communicate the project's success, the CEO and the COO embark on a tour across the country to each of the company's office locations to personally announce the success of the project and the change management that will be expected to keep the new sustainability accomplishments generating value for the company, their customers, and the communities of their office locations.

In discussing complexity and scale, we have made some real headway in the three dimensions associated with problem solving. The last one is a very important dimension that should help you and others understand how dangerous the problem is—or will soon be—to the company.

Severity

Severity is relative to a problem solver's appreciation for the fundamental aspects of a problem and how those fundamental aspects affect the organization.

Is the problem a small bottleneck, a minor drag on the company's efficiency and profitability? Or, is it such a severe problem that the end result, if it isn't solved, will be the ultimate bankruptcy of the company?

As you design your own roadmap to Profitable Problem Solving, you need to score the problem's severity in a present view and in a future view. In other words, how bad is it today, and what will happen if the problem persists? Forecasting severity is important in helping leadership understand exactly what risk you are communicating.

Think back to the GM example. If GM had a system in place that required employees to score the severity of the faulty ignition switches, the current, 2004 score would have been significant enough to solve the problem immediately; but the future score would have been off the charts, since they knew the failure of the ignition switch could lead to airbag failure during a collision or wreck.

Mild

A mild problem is very small and likely has little-to-subtle risk to the company in the near term. To score an issue as mild, you might be solving something that carries less of a hard cost and instead inflicts more of a distraction or annoyance to those who experience the issue. Those issues are still valuable to solve, as you can improve customer satisfaction or employee satisfaction, or gain great testimonials by polishing the rough edges of any process or activity.

Example:

An office manager has decided to work on gaining a supplier discount for shipping. In order to do this, she has to pick one provider and use them for at least 80% of her office's shipping orders. She does her homework, negotiates a fair deal with the provider she thinks is best suited to handle the needs of her company, and signs a new agreement. The total savings per year is measurable, but small. However, she is able to illustrate for management that not only did her decision save shipping costs, but it also increased the employee satisfaction score of the front-door receptionist who will now only have to deal with one company to set up orders and receive incoming packages. The regional manager is so happy with the improvements, she asks the office manager to participate in a conference call with five other offices that will soon be following in her footsteps and making the same changes.

Moderate

Moving beyond the mild category, a moderate problem is important to solve in the near future. Categorizing the severity of your problem as moderate indicates that your problem is contributing to the failure or under-performance of a specific department, division, or subsidiary. Much like you saw with the mid-level categories in the other two dimensions (complexity and scale), moderate severity requires that the problem be unique to a subset of the entire corporation. The common elements shared by the problem make it an important study question for top management, as they have to determine if this problem is a contagious issue that can infect and disrupt other business units. Or, rather, is this problem an isolated issue—kind of a corporate patient-zero scenario—that allows the company to solve it and not worry that the issue will grow to risk the success of the entire organization?

Example:

Grace is a regional vice president for a Tex-Mex restaurant chain with six restaurants in her region. Five of her restaurants are firing at or above all the important key performance indicators (KPIs) for which her division president holds her accountable. One is not. The trouble restaurant is in the Buckhead area of Atlanta, GA. Buckhead is a thriving, competitive area for the hospitality industry. All the market research indicates that their brand should compete very well in Buckhead. Grace travels to the restaurant and has an opportunity to observe much of the lunchtime service before the assistant manager recognizes her in the crowd. Before the assistant manager spots her, she has observed a number of violations of corporate best practices. She notices that the new point of sale (POS) system is not used consistently, and thus the kitchen is getting both system tickets and hand-written orders. She also notices that restaurant cleanliness and low light setting are problems. Those two issues, in combination with other violations she observes, convince her that this is a management issue. Grace meets the assistant manager, who seems to be a one-man show. He is working hard at the bar, the host position, and helping in the kitchen. It seems the general manager is not working the number of hours that have been reported, and thus the restaurant staff have not been trained properly on the new POS system and have not had time to correct schedule issues, and the restaurant has not had regular inspections. Grace decides to make some immediate changes. She hires a new general manager from one of their competitors, who is familiar with their new POS system. She challenges the new manager to clean up the scheduling issues, fix the store, and improve the results. In a few short weeks, the Buckhead restaurant is showing signs of improvement. Months later, the restaurant is one of the top performers in her region.

Severe

A severe problem or group of problems threatens the existence of the company. A problem in this category may call for an enterprise-wide "turnaround," solving a multitude of different problems that are jeopardizing the life of the company.

A truly profound, deep-rooted problem may require "divestiture" of a division or a company, or the removal of a line of business, a division, or a subsidiary that is no longer contributing to the success of the company.

Some people may read divestiture of a business unit as akin to a failure, but this isn't necessarily true. At General Electric, Jack Welch considered divestiture every bit as important as mergers and acquisitions; during the first four years of his tenure as CEO, Welch divested 117 business units. Sandy Weill, while leading the Travelers Group in the 1990s, made 11 significant divestitures; now CEO of Citigroup, he has announced plans to spin off the Travelers Property Casualty business. Richard Wamboid, CEO of specialty-packaging company Pactiv, has sold six businesses since 1999, using the proceeds to strengthen the company's balance sheet and invest in high-growth opportunities. Greg Summe has used divestitures as a tool to transform PerkinElmer from a supplier of low-margin services to the government into an innovative high-tech company.

Example:

In 1984, Disney was the happiest place on Earth — unless you were a Disney shareholder. Disney counted only one cable channel, the Disney Channel, and it was not making money. The only productive assets were the parks and Mickey Mouse licensing, responsible for a rough tax-free cash flow of $100M. Enter Michael Eisner. By 2005, when Eisner left, Disney had grown 32-fold and increased the puny tax-free cash flow to $2.9B, and the stock was flirting with $30. Eisner performed this corporate miracle by leading Disney through wholesale transformation. In addition to adding rigor to the organization and giving the operations a much-needed haircut, he added ABC to the portfolio, which gave Disney 80% of ESPN. In addition to adding valuable, productive acquisitions, he shifted sales from the movie house to the retail storefront and significantly increased the profits from Disney movies. Eisner was successful for many reasons, chief among them that he understood that the Disney he *inherited in 1984 was in jeopardy of losing relevancy, eroding any hope for profitability, and wasting precious resources. His handling of the severe issues that threatened the life of the company would put Disney back on the map.*

Chapter Five

Profitable Problem Solving 101 (Part III)

What is My Score?
The better question is: Is this a problem I can solve?

You don't want to jump into a can of worms, then be embarrassed because you are punching above your weight.

Yes, the sports metaphor was my clever way to make sure you plot a smart path within your company as you identify problems to solve. There will be issues whose score suggests you may not want to tackle them, as they require a level of expertise you have not yet developed. When such a circumstance does arrive, you can still score big points by pointing out issues and providing your support for the solution.

Use this tool like you would plan your day on the slopes. All of us—even those who prefer a hot toddy at the lodge while others are on the slopes—know that beginners ski green, intermediate skiers ski blue, and experts head for the black-diamond runs. No one is going to stop you as you hop on the ski lift to the black-diamond run, but if you want to come down in one piece, you will make sure you pick the run that is right for you.

Problem solving is similar. Instead of using green, blue, and black, let's use a traffic signal to signify when you should go and when you should not.

Green is a go for all problem solvers, new and experienced. Get after it!

Yellow is caution. While some new problem solvers can handle the intricacy, others may park this problem to solve after they have racked up more problem-solving experience.

Red is stop. Really, just stop. Even if you are the entrepreneur who owns 100% of the business, even if you are fully empowered to make transformative initiatives happen, you should make sure you have the right expert at your side. This is a black diamond, and you want to not only solve the problem, but you want to do so without any wipeouts.

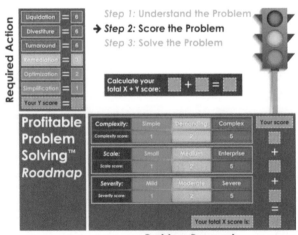

Problem Prognosis

Here is how you figure your score:

Write a brief problem statement that covers the problem matter and the goal of the problem-solving project.

Begin with the X Axis, or the problem prognosis. You have three dimensions. Select one category for each dimension and note the corresponding score.

Total the three scores together to get your total X score.

Now go to the Y Axis and select the action you think is required to solve the problem. Select only one action, and note the corresponding score.

Now add the total score from the X Axis to the total score from the Y Axis and determine what your total score indicates you should do next.

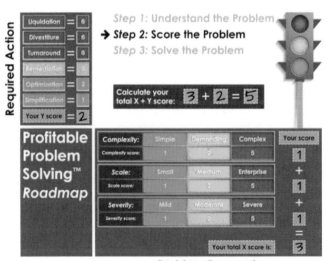

Problem Prognosis

Don't be discouraged if most of your problems are yellow or red. That simply means you have a good eye for trouble.

But do yourself a favor and kick off your career as a problem solver in a smart and strategic way.

Julius Caesar said, "Experience is the teacher of all things." Indeed, use your experience to build your competency in the art of problem solving.

In the example we have mocked up for you, your Y score—or the Requested Action—is Remediation. Your X score—the problem prognosis—is simple, small, and mild, so your total score X score is 3. Add those together, and your Problem Solving Matrix says this is a great problem for you to solve.

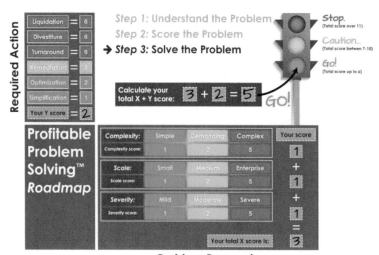

Problem Prognosis

From here forward, we will focus on the strategies for solving the problem and the methods you can use to make sure your successful solution is profitable for you.

CASE STUDY:
McDonald's

I can't think of a corporate icon that has battled more issues over a longer period of time, and yet is still so loved by millions of Americans, as McDonald's. With more than 36,000 restaurants in more than 100 countries serving more than 69 million people — every single day, 365 days a year — McDonald's is the world's largest fast food retailer.

Nearly two million people work for McDonald's or a McDonald's franchise, and most of them come into constant contact with customers. Eighty percent of McDonald's restaurants are franchised, with 11,500 franchise owners balancing dictates from corporate and their own insights into what their local customers want.

So, with all those moving parts, what could go wrong?

Lately, just about everything.

Critics say that McDonald's can't make healthy food and that it can't attract millennials. McDonald's burgers are the worst in the U.S., according to results of a recent reader poll. And McDonald's American Customer Satisfaction Index score, while its best ever, still ranks it at the bottom of the rankings.[9] CEO Don Thompson stepped down in the first quarter of 2015 after two years of declining same-store sales in the United States, where it has lost many customers because of a failure to compete sufficiently with newcomers like Chipotle Mexican Grill.

McDonald's depends on the independent decision making and operational prowess of its franchise owners, and yet it approaches the marketplace with a centralized strategy that allows almost no innovation on the local level.

But turn the history pages back to the early seventies, when annual sales per restaurant doubled and the total number of outlets doubled. The reason? Then-CEO Fred Turner believed McDonald's success was due to empowering employees to solve problems. Turner observed, "The closer decision making is to the stores and the marketplace, the better the decisions that managers make."

Imagine if McDonald's empowered franchise owners to make decisions at the local level and incented franchise owners to post impressive customer service satisfaction scores. And, imagine if point-of-sale sales associates were empowered to solve issues and provide immediate resolution to problems relating to coupons, speed of service, order accuracy, average service time, and time in drive-through (where 70% of McDonald's business happens). I'm willing to bet you'd witness an astonishing turnaround for the world's largest fast food chain.

It doesn't take too much imagination to realize that McDonalds has not yet found the secret sauce for problem solving. Not since Turner's CEO-ship has the company settled on a winning problem-solving strategy. We challenge McDonalds to reach back into their earlier play book and renew their perspective on empowering people and growing their business based on the talents of those empowered by their strong culture and brand.

Chapter Six

Problem Statement

Looking for Trouble

Now that you have an appreciation for Problem Solving 101 and the tools needed to dig in and solve problems, from the simple to the complex, let's keep moving and discuss the six important steps you'll need to solve problems successfully.

Every industry benefits from the economy in a slightly different manner. Some industries are leading indicators of an economic shift, while other industries are lagging indicators of a shift. The impact of GDP, oil, gold, and interest rates can hit an industry hard and fast, or they can sneak up on the industry over a slow but certain roll. The point here is that your career will likely take you through a number of different economic cycles. You will love the ups and dread the downs, but fortunately for you, both the bear and the bull markets offer companies plenty of problems—and thus, they offer you plenty of opportunity.

You will have plenty of chances to solve problems confronting your company, gain a reputation as a problem solver, and promote your own achievements. As a good friend of mine used to say during sales trainings, "Don't leave the sizzle in the pan."

Start Simple

The best problems to solve, when you are new to the problem-solving routine, are inefficiencies. An inefficiency will register as either a simplification or optimization activity on our Profitable Problem Solving™ Scale.

These are processes that are not really broken. Rather, you're simply taking something that isn't operating as well as it could and tuning it up.

Simplifying an inefficiency creates less disruption than reinventing an existing process or creating a new one. Trust me, you're less likely to encounter strong resistance when you start with problems that are easy to solve and offer tangible value to the company. This is the ideal way to practice problem solving.

"But what is there to practice?" you might ask.

You've identified your problem, analyzed your trends, and developed your solution. Easy, right?

Well, no.

Problem solving is a skill that requires practice to perfect. It doesn't always come naturally, even to the brightest, most talented people.

I have friends who are incredible athletes. Professional athletes, even. But just because someone is an awesome performer in one sport doesn't mean she'll easily master another.

The same applies to you in your career. "I'm smart, I've got that degree or training, I'm doing great in my job." But every new role, in life or sports or work, requires practice to perfect. You're better off starting with a relatively easy challenge before moving on to something earth shattering.

For that reason, smoothing out inefficiencies is a great place to start. Take a 360° look around your office, your shop floor, or your division. All you have to do is ask, "What's slowing me down?" Right there, you've identified an inefficiency that needs tuning up. And even though inefficiencies may seem to be relatively minor, it is often the case that some small glitch, once solved—and especially if it's Factor 10'd across offices and shops and regions—can yield incredible value to the company.

And, in yielding value to the company, it should create benefit for you, the entrepreneurial problem solver.

What is the Winning Combination?

Much as you would try to structure your investment portfolio, you want to get the highest return for the lowest amount of risk. If you have an investment idea that favors buying the equity (stock) in one company, you'd better be sure you are making a great decision. While the fundamentals and the market info may make it seem like a diamond in the rough, you are sure to have plenty of options offering a similar return in a fund or diverse product that teases out the risk of one company and replaces it with the reward from the performance of the collective.

Don't get me wrong, I am not an investment professional and am absolutely not giving you investment advice. However, no matter your risk tolerance, getting a higher return for less risk is a guiding principle for investors. It is a good one for problem solvers to adopt, as well. If you just look at the possible return and do not take into consideration the risk you are taking, you will be left to sort out the mess in the end if your premise had a flaw or the market had a hiccup.

So in our problem-solving world, solving a simple problem (because it has the highest probability of success), a problem with a green light combined with a future view of severity that categorizes the problem as moderate or severe, is a high-value option that we can refer to as the sweet spot. The challenge is to find one of these gems, as most problems that yield a green light today will probably have a present view of severity and a future view of severity that are pretty consistent. In other words, most problems that are simple and small will not likely grow to be a threat to a business unit or the entire company. But here is the thing, there are sure to be a couple of them that can if left unresolved.

If your problem includes any of the following issues, make sure you have truly considered the future impact to the company. Ask yourself the following questions about each issue, considering its potential, if left unresolved, to grow into a bigger issue:

Safety. Can the issue harm, or contribute to some harm, to our customers or the general public? If not today, can that prognosis change in the future?

Environment. Can the issue harm or modify the environment? If not today, can that prognosis change in the future?

Quality. Will the quality of our product or service deteriorate if this issue persists?

Discrimination and Fairness. Does this problem result in some type of unfair advantage for one group of employees, customers, shareholders, or strategic partners? Conversely, does it put one group of employees, customers, shareholders, or strategic partners in an unfair disadvantage?

Relevancy. Is this issue threatening our brand's relevancy in the market? If not today, is it probable to fear we can be replaced in the future by a superior technology or competitor?

Profitability. Does this problem result in the waste of our resources? If left unresolved, will the cost rise?

Brand Integrity. Does this issue conflict with our core values? If left unresolved, would the social impact of the problem create a public backlash toward our brand?

Compliance and Regulations. Does this problem create a violation of any municipal, state, or federal laws? Does it violate any regulatory or supervisory requirement that we must obey? If the problem exists in an international realm, does it create a violation of any law or standard that we must comply with today?

Security. Does this issue put our corporate data, our customer's sensitive data, or other trade secret documentation at risk for security breach? If the problem is mitigated now but not completely solved, what is the future risk and timeline?

Yes, there are other questions you can ask, but this is a list of questions you can ask with every problem you plan to solve. The answers will help you determine how rapidly the risk will grow if you leave the problem to be solved another day.

What About Yellow? How Can I be Both Bold and Cautious?

Two quick things to remember when looking at the problems designated as "ready for the experienced problem solver."

First, one of the clear indicators of a challenging problem is that the action required to solve the problem is remediation, instead of the two simpler options, optimization or simplification. Remember, remediation requires you to plan to "fix" the issue. This means you have to think about a number of critical matters. First, does the solution you have devised solve the problem? If yes, what does it do to the people up and downstream of your solution? Does your solution result in a win for your department but confusion for the rest of the company? Consider the sales manager who, in efforts to gain another hour of prospecting time, reduced the amount of information his sales reps were required to input into the company's CRM system. Great, he was able to get his sales reps back on sales calls five minutes faster by adjusting the information they provided about the deal they had just closed. Two weeks later, the sales manager received an angry call from the VP of Finance & Accounting, because the lack of information in the CRM system resulted in a number of billing discrepancies with new customers—all very frustrated with the experience they were having with their new service provider.

Don't make the same mistake. Before you remedy a problem by changing or re-engineering a process, make sure you know what it means to the other key departments and functions in your company.

And Red Still Means Stop?

Yes, just stop and do not attempt unless you have the right authority, approval, and expertise.

CASE STUDY:
General Motors and Mary Barra

Problems are almost always less expensive to ignore than to fix — at least in the very short term — but they have a way of gaining traction and becoming enormous problems.

Long before Mary Barra became General Motors' CEO in January 2014, the company knew about faulty ignition switches, which could slip out of position, unexpectedly cutting power to brakes, steering, and airbags. The defect has been linked to 160 injuries and 80 deaths. Back in 2004, GM engineers knew about the defect and its potential for tragedy, but the culture of the company was such that engineers "made the problem go away," rather than solving it. They did what the company expected of them, and GM didn't face up to the problem and begin recalling vehicles until 2014.

GM cars had already been on the road with those faulty switches for a decade. GM has recalled 2.6 million vehicles, but it's far too late for those 80 fatalities and their families. The Barra has set up a victim's compensation fund that had approved 64 claims as of Q1 2015, and GM estimates that the fund will ultimately pay out over $600 million in claims.

How different could things have been if GM had cultivated a culture that rewarded its engineers for fixing the faulty ignition switch before it went into production?

Would GM and its customers have benefited from a culture in which employees were encouraged to identify problems and advance solutions when they were still small and manageable? You be the judge.

As GM emerges from their bankruptcy and begins to show growth in profits and plans to expand investment — $9 billion in capital spending per year [11] — they must invest in their people and culture to ensure that the next ignition switch issue (metaphorically speaking) is solved on the line and not in the news.

Chapter Seven

Research Trends

Build Your Case

Problem solvers, even highly experienced problem solvers, often overlook Step Two of the six-step process. Don't kid yourself, making the time to *research trends* and understand the depth of an issue is a huge part of creating a successful plan—and an even bigger part of how you will later forecast the value your solution will bring the company (and then, of course, your reward).

If you think about it, you probably wouldn't make a big career move without doing some research, so it stands to reason that you should also research each problem you seek to solve and add to your portfolio.

Each time you identify and set out to solve a problem—whether it's the simple, small, mild problem you tackle first, or a more difficult problem you address later in your profitable problem solving career—set yourself up for success by **identifying trends** relating to the problem. Once you have data (even a small amount), you can begin to see how problem-specific trends will help you diagnose what type of action is required.

Recall the Y axis of our Profitable Problem Solving Roadmap™. With the data you collect, you can begin to discern if the particular task is more difficult or time-consuming than it needs to be; that is, you'll see if it's a great candidate for *simplification*.

Or, the trends may point you in a slightly different direction, suggesting that the business process you are examining requires *optimization*.

With sufficient data to build a significant and plausible case, you can dig into the three key dimensions of your problem (*complexity, scale, and severity*) and determine whether this is a problem you should even tackle. Assuming your problem score gives you the green light for a go, you can move forward and plan to deal with the specifics of your problem.

If you doubt the importance or ubiquitous nature of data trends, make sure you dig into the sports-related case study at the end of this chapter. I picked this case study as a result of my son's contributions to my research. He is what most people would call a sports fan extraordinaire. Since he was a small boy, he was able to tell you the stats for almost any player in nearly every sport. As he grew into a young man, he turned that passion into an opportunity to blog and write about sports-related issues and events. It was not a surprise that while I was researching this book, he suggested I dust off my copy of *Moneyball* and use it to illustrate the value of data in a problem-solving exercise. He was right; there isn't a better example of how data can both support your solution and become a key part of your solution.

What are Trends?

The Internet is littered with blogs and newsletters regarding the next big index of trends in business, social media, financial markets, currency rates, the jobless rate, and on and on. Here is the point for you to remember: If it is important, someone is measuring it.

I remember my first big introduction to my father's handyman skills. He was visiting for a few weeks and decided to help me out by building a customized shoe rack for my closet. What a great idea. I decided to help him and tackle the task father-daughter-style. I grabbed the saw, and he laughed as he took it out of my hands and handed me a tape measure. I immediately assumed he had not noticed that I had already measured the board and marked where I would cut. I was wrong. He had a lesson for me that went way beyond that shelf we were building. He said that my grandpa had taught him an important lesson, and he was passing it on to me: "Measure twice, cut once."

Now, I am not suggesting you need to use mad mathematical skills and apply a complex statistical model to your effort. On the contrary, I designed this book to give you a proxy for the most academic concepts in problem solving so that you can focus more on the issue than the process.

How Do I Get Started?

First, decide how you will document your trends. I suggest using Excel. It is quick and easy. Also, it is easy to share your data points with your leadership team, should they want to formalize your project. Don't panic if you are not comfortable with Excel. Spend fifteen minutes on Viddywise or YouTube, and you will find numerous experts who offer quick videos on getting started with Excel. Until you get into yellow problems, a basic working knowledge of Excel is more than sufficient. If you are still not convinced, feel free to be as basic as jotting down your data points in a notebook. We will make it work. You bring the data, and the process I am sharing here will help you handle the rest.

Okay, now that we have a place to put the data, let's decide what type of data you should collect. Here is a down-and-dirty way to figure out what data points you might want to collect. We'll address two main categories and leave the rest for the MBA. First, let's do a quick statistics review. I promise this is as complicated as the process becomes.

A *variable* is essentially a number or value. There are two types of variables you will want to use: dependent variables and independent variables. The *independent variable* is the thing that causes your *dependent variable* to change. Think of the *independent variable* as the cause and—yes, you guessed it—the *dependent variable* is your effect. Simple, right? Let's put this into action with a simple test:

Example:

Sally, a branch manager, is trying to reduce the amount of overtime her company is paying to contractors as a part of her goal to reduce expenses and optimize profits. She has noticed that contractors who claim more than eight hours in a day are billing for time spent commuting to and from the office. She estimates that out of the total overtime, commuter hours represent at least thirty percent of the total outflow of overtime dollars.

She then determines that the next biggest contributor to overtime cost comes from the time spent putting together expense reports and documenting receipts, as this represents a quarter of total overtime payments.

Wow! Slightly more than 50% of overtime dollars are paying for time that the agreement with all contractors explicitly states can't be billed for; rather, they are expected to commute and seek reimbursement of expenses on their own time. As Sally begins to organize the data she has collected, she notes that the commuter time and expense reconciliation time is causing an unacceptable rise in overtime payouts.

Armed with this data, Sally builds her plan to cut overtime costs in half. As Sally reduces the amount of labor expenses for the branch, she has dollars that now drop straight to her profit line.

Did you see the way the variables worked together and why Sally selected those data points? She could have collected hundreds of other facts, but these important trends supported her belief that overtime was eroding profits. She will not only use these facts to support her plan to adjust the hours billed by contractors, but she will also use the trends to calculate the amount of savings and thus the value of her project. Once she uses Factor 10 Results™ to scale those results across her region and then entire company, Sally will have an impressive win on her hands and a great case for helping her boss justify Sally's promotion to regional manager.

You can collect data as easily as Sally did. For example, how many hours does it take to complete certain tasks, how much overtime do you approve, or how many customers complain about certain products or services? Alternatively, you can use sources of information easily found online to provide big-picture trends, such as GDP, corporate profits, or spending from certain customer segments. Either way, whether you collect your data directly or indirectly, your problem solution must use trends to accomplish the following requisites in profitable problem solving:

Validate that the problem is real and ongoing;

Provide support for the problem-solving plan; and

Create a baseline for status quo and a basis for forecasting the value of the future solution.

Now that you've collected the data, how do you measure trends?

Measuring trends is like exercising. There are lots of experts out there ready to tell you the right way to complete each activity. Yes, indeed, fitness trainers help people achieve some ambitious health goals with their special blend of activities and rigorous schedules. However, there is something to be said for just showing up to the gym and putting in a good 30 minutes of cardio and 30 minutes of muscle-building exercises. If you do this three times a week, you will likely improve your health, fitness, and happiness.

Measuring trends is similar. If you commit to collecting the data and making comparisons on a regular basis, you will make a good start on a successful project. If you are going to take the route without a coach (someone in your leadership team to guide you to the right metrics), make sure your analysis includes the following:

Create a baseline. What are the current trends that result from the problem? In other words, if not for your solution, what will the data continue to show?

Gains/Savings. Does your solution create a gain in sales, profits, customers, or some other important measure that you can quantify? If not, what about savings? Will your solution save money or time?

Comparison to baseline. Compare your new data points to your baseline to determine how much value you are creating for the company.

Here are some additional comparisons that your leadership will be interested in:

Compare to the previous year

Compare changes year over year

Compare to an average year (or longer time period)

How Complicated Does the Analysis Have to Be?

If you can't tell just yet, one of the themes of this book is *keep it simple.* The goals of your analysis should include validating your problem and creating a baseline for calculating future value. The less you complicate this effort, the easier it will be to get buy-in from your management team when you present your solution. I promise, sticking with a simple analysis that justifies your premise and clearly illustrates value is much better than introducing a complicated spreadsheet that no one can follow. You don't want to find yourself on the spot, defending your numbers, instead of talking about the future value of your problem-solving project.

CASE STUDY:
Billy Beane and *Moneyball*

The New York Yankees and the Boston Red Sox are famous for buying their way to success (which doesn't make me any less of a Yankees fan). The Yankees and the Red Sox regularly top the major leagues in opening day roster salaries (often more than $200,000,000), and their league championships and World Series championships were taken as proof that buying the very best talent, as identified by the teams' highly skilled scouts, was the path to victory on the diamond.

But Billy Beane, general manager of the Oakland A's, was handicapped by leading a team with one of the lowest roster salaries in major league baseball. In this stat, the A's ranked 27th out of 30 teams, spending about $86M per year. Distressed at a loss to the Yankees in the 2001 playoffs, Beane was further upset to watch three of the A's free-agent stars lured away by higher paychecks. Beane wondered if there was another way.

Beane met Peter Brand, a Yale economics graduate with a unique approach to evaluating players. Professional scouts typically used a heavy dose of intuition to identify baseball superstars, but Brand's data-based algorithm combined players' on-base percentage (OBP) statistic with an array of little-used stats. The purpose of his analysis was to identify otherwise undervalued players. Brand's method identified players who had been rejected by scouts, but who Brand believed — and Beane came to believe, too — could do great things for the A's.

Beane used Brand's unorthodox statistical analysis to fill the A's 2002 with "rejects."

The A's season started off unevenly, but as these misfits began to learn to play together (and after Beane traded away the last "traditional" player on the roster), they improved. Eventually, during one remarkable stretch of the season, the A's would win 20 consecutive games, an all-time American League record.

Well, that's a great baseball story, isn't it? But what does it have to do with profitable problem solving?

The bestselling book about Billy Beane's triumph with the A's — Michael Lewis's *Moneyball: The Art of Winning an Unfair Game* — and the movie "Moneyball," starring Brad Pitt, have become indelibly etched into the consciousness of an entire generation of young business executives. Creative data analysis has become part of the exec's toolkit, encouraging entrepreneurial businesspeople to use data to challenge conventional wisdom, exploit inefficiencies, and allocate resources in unexpected, but highly productive and profitable, ways.

We're all ballplayers now!

Chapter Eight

Outline Your Solution

Plan for Success

Step Three is an exciting part of your journey. It is time to **build a plan** that will solve the problem and create value.

By now you likely have some exciting problems ready for the plan-building process. What will you do? Will you add a new process to an accounting procedure, so you can close the books a day sooner and push your reporting closer to real time for executives? Will you change the way people submit payable requests to the accounting department to help decrease days payable outstanding (DPO)? Or will you change the location of tools on the manufacturing floor, saving workers time-consuming steps and the company valuable productivity? Whatever the solution, it is time to build your plan.

What Does a Winning Plan Include?

Your plan must include a few basic elements to comprehensively set you for success. Note that some of the steps we mention here will be outlined in greater detail in future chapters.

To make this section simple to follow, let's imagine you are a sales manager for a company that provides Internet marketing solutions to small- and mid-size businesses. Your company offers four primary products: The Brand Building Package, The Email Marketing Package, The Search Engine Optimization Package, and the Social Media Package. One customer could benefit from buying every product, but your customer data indicate that only 35% of your customers own three or more products, and only 50% of your customers own two products. Management has given you the goal of increasing sales by 10%, but of course, you can't hire more salespeople to hit the new target.

Since you are a smart problem solver, you follow the right steps and decide that in order to solve the problem, you must improve cross-selling (sales to existing customers of complimentary products or services) and increase the number of customers who own multiple products. Makes sense, right? These customers already have at least one of your products, and it's a good bet that they are happy, since they are still paying for the monthly service.

After doing your homework, your plan begins to take shape. As you build your plan, you make sure to include the right planning elements. Let's take a look at which of these planning components are a must (critical) and which ones you can consider more discretionary (optional):

Problem Statement (critical). A general statement of the problem and the consequence to the organization.

Example:

Your sales process has a heavy focus on closing cold calls made by your inside sales team within your target segments. The inside sales team has ten sales reps who are making over 100 dials a day and closing nearly 30% of all outbound calls.

The inside sales team must generate a net increase of 10% in the next three months in order to hit sales targets. Without an adjustment in the sales strategy, the 10% increase will not likely happen, as the team is operating

above productivity metrics and you are unable to obtain the
approval for new staff.

Solution Statement (critical). A general statement outlining the goals and the benefit of the solution.

Example:

Effective immediately, sales will kick off a cross-selling initiative. All salespeople will receive training to quickly learn the goals of a new cross-selling script, and they will begin to call customers to whom your company has sold products in the past year; their goal is to sell at least one more product to each customer. To preclude cannibalizing new sales, the sales day will be split up, and each sales representative will continue the usual cold-calling strategy for 75% of her active calls planned. The remaining 25% of her calls will be directed toward existing customers for the cross-selling initiative. The cross-selling initiative will extend a 10% savings to existing customers who buy on the first cross-selling call. The discounted margin is still about the 32% required limit.

Your Motivation for Solving this Problem (critical). This is your opportunity to lay the groundwork for the personal gain you will seek for a job well done on this project (and future projects in your portfolio). The motivation should be stated in a win-win manner.

Example:

Remember early in the book, I shared a story about how I pitched a solution for the company I was working for during Y2K and was rewarded because the project was a win-win for the company and myself?

Well, let me clarify. I did not say to the division president in my presentation, "and after I do all of these incredible things, I expect a promotion, a raise, and exciting new challenges" (even though that is what I indeed received). No. Instead, I included in my presentation a slide that covered, in just a few words, my motivation for this extraordinary endeavor: 1) being a team player; 2) relying on my work ethic to do my best; and 3) a belief that as I do good things for the company, the company will do good things for me. I used that last bullet as a springboard to gain new responsibility, a promotion, and an increase in compensation as my problem-solving portfolio grew.

Supporting Data (critical). A general statement about the data or trends that validate your problem diagnosis and support your solution approach.

Example:

Sales is currently generating $1,900,000 with ten reps. Each sales representative has an annual quota of $150,000, which is an industry standard. All ten of your sales representatives have already met or are on track to meet their quota for this fiscal year. Therefore, you can't expect a 10% increase out of the same team without some drastic changes.

The good news is that you know from your client data that your existing customers are mostly happy with your services, and most only own one of your products. You believe that the calls will be faster, since the sales representatives have already established a relationship and the discount will entice the customer to buy more of your products.

Currently, representatives close about $600 of new business a day to stay on track with their quota. To achieve an increase of 10% in sales, the new cross-selling requirements should push the average sales toward $700 per day. We think this is possible for three months.

Additional Data (optional). Include budget or analysis conducted to further validate your problem diagnosis and support your solution approach.

Cost Forecast (Critical). Forecast of cost for the entire project.

Example:

The cost of training will be exceptionally low. The plan is to order pizza for the team twice in one week to conduct a brown-bag training session. Cost = $200.

The remaining costs are indirect and associated with the time to generate the new script. The time to generate the scripts can be off-peak and thus not costly.

Value (critical). Forecast of value for the project once successfully completed.

Example:

A 10% increase in sales would generate $150,000 in net new revenue. The new annual sales revenue would exceed $1,650,000.

Factor 10 Results™ (critical). Scale the value of the solution to illustrate enterprise-wide value.

Example:

After a quarter of successfully achieving a growth in sales, the hiring plan for the sales team can be expanded from the current headcount of 10 to 15. A sales team operating within the same productivity metrics would generate sales of $2,625,000. That is an increase of $875,000 per year. The addition of five new salespeople will not change the floor plan of the office or the number of managers needed to manage the team, which makes the cost of their salary and benefits a pretty good deal when you look at the expected new revenue.

Project Timeline (optional). List the amount of time and key milestones in the project. This is particularly important for projects that will last more than three months.

Next steps (critical). The next steps needed to launch project.

Example:

The next steps include building the script, conducting the two training sessions, and then launching the new call schedule. These steps can be completed in one week, and you can be selling more products one week from today.

Does Every Great Plan Need a Plan B?

I learned in business school that the answer to almost every question is, "It depends."

So, do you need a plan B? It depends, but most probably you do.

You are most prepared when you have a **next best alternative** in your pocket.

"What's that about?" you might ask. "I'm proposing the perfect solution."

Well, that may be true, but let's be realistic. Plan B is part of a comprehensive strategy for problem solving. It is your hedge against management's possible objection to risk or cost. Imagine your primary plan as the fully loaded version (full of optimal outcome); a next best alternative (iterative results, less risk) is the back up, available when your management team objects to the size, cost, timing, or feasibility of your plan. This gives you options.

Options cannot be overrated. If you want to stack the deck in your favor, ask for permission to do A or B, not just, *"Can we move forward with Project A?"* Anyone who has sold a deal knows that asking *if* the prospect would like to buy the product is much more difficult than asking *which* product the prospect would like to buy.

Imagine your scenario. You may announce, "Hey, here are the trends that prove we have a problem. I'm going to solve it, and here's how I'm going to do it!" But until you are a proven problem solver with the ear of the CEO, you won't have earned the total, perfect confidence of your supervisors and your colleagues. And, no matter how perfect your plan, it involves some level of risk. Despite your best effort, the possibility exists that your proposal is going to get a *"Nice try, but no."*

So, you should have a next best alternative up your sleeve.

I call this "the pony strategy."

Imagine a clever child who starts pestering her parents, "I want a pony. Please, can I have a pony?"

"No way are we getting a pony," says the mom. "We don't have room for a pony. We'd have to build a barn. We'd have to buy bales of hay."

The child pesters, and pesters, and drives mom and dad half crazy about this damn pony.

But then one day, the child says, "Well, how about a kitten?"

After all this business of the pony, a kitten seems like a totally reasonable alternative. "Sure, sweetheart, we'll get you a kitten."

The child would have liked a pony. What child wouldn't? But she's pretty happy with her next best alternative: a cuddly little kitten.

So, I suggest you ask for a pony, but be prepared to suggest a kitten.

Propose the perfect solution, but be ready with a less risky way to address the problem.

Give management an option other than "yes" or "no," and you may walk away with approval for a "pretty good" solution. And that's a lot better than nothing.

Yes, we are almost done with planning. As we wrap up your new plan, make sure you include the next important planning steps that you must do in conjunction with building an actual project plan. The following planning steps can be the difference between a flop and a true victory.

Build the Right Team

If you are working on a simple, small, mild problem, the sort of problem that is totally inside your area of responsibility, then it makes a lot of sense to solve it yourself—as a lone wolf—creating the value and reaping the benefits.

But for most problem solving, I believe the concept of lone wolf is a little bit stifling. If you are solving your own problems and you're the only one benefiting from the solutions, then you're not going to stir up much interest or create much excitement.

Most of us, except for the sole proprietor running her own company, exist in an environment where our actions impact others. We depend on others to get anything done. In this environment, the lone wolf is going to starve.

So, in most cases, except in dealing with the simplest of issues, you'll be involving colleagues.

Before putting together a taskforce or team, you independently identified the problem, gathered and analyzed the relevant trends, put the outlines of your solution into writing, and have begun the final steps of problem solving before making the big proposal to management. This is where the team (assuming your solution is *medium* or *enterprise* in *scale*) comes into play.

Some problem solvers that are new to project management worry that they will not have the right type of respect from the team due to their lack of experience. Don't worry, between the Factor 10 Reach concepts you will learn and the hard work you have already invested in the effort, you'll easily be recognized as the champion of this project.

You can increase the likelihood your new leadership skills are received well by your team if you are a collegial, respectful leader; but, by all means, be the leader. Be the communicator. Turn your team into a rock band—and you're the lead singer!

Build the Right Audience

Your next step is to **build the right audience.**

Building the right audience is essential for two reasons.

First, of course, the right audience helps to move obstacles out of your way, easing your path to become an effective change-agent.

If the problem you've identified lies outside your own area, it is essential to build the right audience so you have the support to move forward. Otherwise, if you begin suggesting problems and solutions that impact people outside your area, even with the best intentions, you are sure to find yourself stepping on toes. The experience can turn on a dime, from a profitable one into a disaster.

Simplification and optimization can be done by one person, but as you go up the scale—to remediation, turnaround, divestiture, and liquidation—the the action required to address the problem or collection of problems is going to disrupt other employees. There's no way around it. Such extreme actions are going to cause pain, there will be resistance, and you will find yourself swimming against the tide. However, if you've brought the right people into the process, their support will help you get the job done.

Building the right audience also ensures that you will profit from your problem-solving initiative. In the best of all possible worlds, each of us would get credit for every great deed we accomplish. Unfortunately, as you may have noticed, this is something less than that ideal world. There are pirates and vultures everywhere. Share your great idea with the wrong people, and you may find it stolen right out from under you. But if you carefully build your audience, use the concepts in Factor 10 Results™ to include the *Reach* that covers your original efforts, and establish your plan with them, you will anchor yourself as the key problem solver.

Then, when you go to report your results, you can rest assured that the problem-solving initiative will belong to you. Credit will be given where credit is deserved—to *you*.

CASE STUDY:
Adam Kutac

Adam Kutac is not your typical superhero. Bow-tied and bespectacled, he seems too mild-mannered to move mountains. I wonder if people said the same thing about young Clark Kent.

While studying pre-med at the University of St. Thomas in Houston, Adam realized that a career as a doctor would be lucrative, but his heart just wasn't in it. His passion was thinking, writing, and teaching others to think and write. He earned a B.A. degree in child psychology, philosophy, and creative writing, passed his state teacher's certification exams, and landed in the Houston Independent School District, the seventh largest school district in the United States. He began his career as a third-grade teacher.

A sobering fact about teaching in an inner-city school district is that typically upwards of 75% of the students are at or below the poverty line, so teachers deal not only with the usual challenges of getting kids excited about math, science, and history, but they also must navigate the very real socio-economic issues that often interfere with a student's interest in learning. Just as distressing to Adam: he soon learned that the teaching milieu in which he'd landed was based on his pupils' success on standardized tests, rather than on what they actually learned.

Adam decided that "teaching to the test" would short-change his students. He decided that teaching his students to think critically about multiplication, social studies, and the world around them would be better for his students in the long run, and it was a better approach to success on the standardized exams, too. He analyzed the approved curriculum and designed creative ways to engage his students in math, science, English, and history.

The test results were stunning.

Every single one of Adam's students passed the test in both math and reading. It was the first time in the school's history that an entire classroom of students had passed both tests.

That early success has helped shape a career that took Adam from teacher to assistant principal in just short eight years. Adam is founding assistant principal at KIPP Connect Primary, a new school in Houston that is part of the Knowledge Is Power Program (KIPP). While only eight percent of students from low-income communities across the nation graduate from college, KIPPsters boast a 54 percent college graduation rate.

Adam attributes his personal success to five key ingredients, all of which were evident in that experience with his third-grade class: he was doing something he was passionate about, he kept an open mind, he relied on his instincts, he remained open and coachable as a mentee, and he modeled that behavior for his students.

In his current work, Adam has had to solve a lot of problems: finding ways to keep teachers and students motivated and engaged in the learning process, while creating and sustaining systems and processes that will serve the school as it continues to grow. When identifying problems, gauging their complexity, and going about the work of building coalitions and support for solving them, Adam always comes back to those five key things that helped him make history for his school while instilling lasting intellectual habits and a love for learning in that early class of students. His goal is to continue to use his powers for good and replicate that success every single day for the rest of his career.

Just days before this book goes to press — exciting news! Adam has been promoted to principal of the KIPP Connect Primary.

Chapter Nine

Forecast Cost

Be Smart with Resources

The reality of almost every solution is that there is a cost associated with the effort. Nothing good comes to you for free, it seems.

While the best-case scenario for every project is that it can be held to a cost-neutral standard (said more plainly, it brings in more value than it costs), that does not always happen. And while that can be achieved in a few circumstances, you can't always assume perfect timing.

What do I mean by perfect timing? I am prepping you for the fact that your company may have to invest in the solution first and wait for a period of time for the return on investment. Since the capital outlay usually comes before the value, you have to do a good job of identifying the costs so no one in your organization is surprised.

Even when you can claim the trophy for a cost-neutral project, you still must identify the costs involved in the project so that the company can track the progress and hold you accountable to the net return you are predicting.

How Do I Forecast Something with Accuracy?

That is an age-old accounting question. Financial managers are forever working to tighten up their forecast so that it more closely matches the actuals that will later be used in analysis. But hey, let's keep this simple and focus on the due diligence you need to do in project planning.

To forecast cost, let's begin by identifying direct costs and indirect costs. Direct costs are the costs your company incurs to produce a product or service. They may take the form of materials or labor. Indirect costs are a little different; these are costs that your company incurs as a result of doing business, such as advertising, security, and technology. Why am I going into this level of cost detail? Simply put, if you only forecast your direct costs, you will underestimate the true cost to the company.

Example:

Matthew's company produces furniture. When Matthew looks at the direct costs of building the furniture, he counts the wood, nails, glue, varnish, and carpenters. He knows these are direct costs because he can attach these costs directly to the production of his product.

Matthew has other costs, as well. When he calculates the indirect costs, he includes his office rent, the warehouse, and the security officers he hires to keep the property and inventory safe. He knows these are indirect costs because, while important, the rent and warehouse costs are not a direct cost of the production.

Let me say this: If you don't separate your costs into a direct cost line and an indirect cost line, it is not the end of the world. In this book, I am speaking to a problem solvers with varied experience and a huge range of accounting skills. The key message: Do what make sense to you. The goal is to use these steps to formalize and polish your planning to gain a successful outcome.

Look at these categories and decide if they will be helpful in identifying the costs your project will incur:

Examples of Direct Costs:

Labor: Salary or hourly rates of people dedicated to the project.

Subcontract: Third party services.

Materials: Cost of items you must utilize in the project plan.

Travel: Planes, trains, and automobiles.

Examples of Indirect Costs:

Employee benefits: Benefits (including health insurance, life insurance, sick and holiday leave, 401K contributions). Hint—this is in addition to labor costs you listed in your direct cost column.

General & administrative: A measured portion of the salaries of others who contribute indirectly to your project (the IT Helpdesk, telephone reception).

Rent & Premise Expenses: Office space.

Equipment: Tools and technology.

As you start thinking about the project, you want to make sure you capture the right costs.

Your next step is to determine how much you will really spend in the categories you identified. Is it 20 hours a week? Or rather, is it 30 hours a week? The difference between the two can blow your budget it you are not careful.

Once you have the costs captured, you should document them. As I suggested before, I recommend you use Excel. Assuming your project is a great candidate for the company to replicate, the senior financial executives will utilize these costs to make sure the company has properly accounted and allocated the costs to the right department. There are some costs that the accounting team can expense and some that they may opt to capitalize. Knowing the accounting treatment shouldn't be a worry for you in the planning stages, but you should be aware that it is part of what a company will consider when greenlighting or killing a new investment.

I had a large project that I introduced early in my career that was so well received it ultimately went to the CEO and CFO for final approval. The plan was to build a new software product for a thriving consulting practice so the firm could compete with advantage over other service companies that did not have their own intellectual property. The project costs were acceptable, until the CFO did some research and learned that GAAP (generally accepted accounting principles) would not allow him to capitalize the expense of building the program until we could produce a working prototype.

Translation? The company would have to expense the costs. Put another way, the company would have to use dollars that could have been profit to pay for the early stages of production. Once we had a working prototype, GAAP would allow the company to capitalize the costs and thus treat them differently on the financials.

Why am I telling you this? Because I was not prepared to hear that everyone thought this was a great idea, *BUT* we would have to wait a year to do it so it could be built into the next year fiscal budget.

In reality, we did not wait. We found a customer willing to sponsor the development, and we were able to adjust the financial impact to be more affordable to the CFO. You may end up horse trading to keep your solution on track, as well.

Make Sure You Plan to Track Costs During the Project

As part of planning for costs, you should plan to track costs. It is one thing to say you think the project will cost $100. Even better to go back after the project and claim a victory because your project really did cost $100 or less. Or rather, if you didn't mange it well or properly forecast costs in the beginning, prepare to explain why it cost more than you projected.

One way you might want to track cost is to keep a running inventory of costs that you and your team incur. If you have expense reporting forms or guidelines your firm uses, consider having the project listed as a project code so the accounting team can track those expenses for you as your team turns in their expenses. If you do not have that luxury, consider the following options:

Status reports with a section for identifying costs incurred and costs pending

Excel-based reporting

Quickbooks

Expense tracking apps for your mobile device available online

Build in the Budget Numbers

By forecasting the project costs, you have done the hard part. Now you need to drop those future costs into a budget. The budget can get complicated, but why? The goal of the budget is to document the financial plan for the entire project. You already looked at the direct and indirect costs. The last step is an easy way to button up this section of you plan.

If you are not sure what format to drop the budget into, never fear. Your friend Google can provide a myriad of options. Again, as you select your option, try not to complicate the effort, as you will have to track costs and report your performance against the budget you publish. Something as simple as the example below can get most projects going; it's easy enough to change the cost inputs if the examples in the template I have provided are wrong for you. Simply replace them with the ones you have already forecasted.

Project Budget Template

	Direct Costs				Indirect Costs				Total
	Labor	Sub-contractors	Materials	Travel	Benefits Paid Leave	G & A	Premise	Equipment	
January									
February									
March									
April									
May									
June									
July									
August									
September									
October									
November									
December									
FY Total									
Percentage of Total									

After you begin to drop in some of your numbers, the budget will begin to take shape and become a tool you will use to track accountability and success. Here is second look at the template with some mock project budget numbers included.

Project Budget Template

	Direct Costs				Indirect Costs				Total
	Labor	Sub-con-tractors	Materials	Travel	Benefits fat load	G & A	Premise	Equipment	
January	$14,500	$8,080	$2,000	$8,200	$5,625	$1,010	$3,500	$3,500	$46,335
February	$14,800	$8,080	$1,800	$8,200	$5,625	$1,010	$3,500	$3,500	$48,835
March	$15,000	$8,080	$4,100	$8,200	$5,750	$1,010	$3,500	$3,500	$49,040
April	$14,800	$8,080	$7,100	$8,200	$5,625	$1,010	$3,500	$3,500	$51,435
May	$14,800	$8,080	$4,100	$8,200	$5,625	$1,010	$3,500	$3,500	$48,435
June	$15,000	$8,080	$1,500	$8,200	$5,750	$1,010	$3,500	$3,500	$46,460
July	$14,500	$8,080	$1,500	$8,200	$5,625	$1,010	$3,500	$3,500	$43,835
August	$14,500	$8,080	$1,500	$8,200	$5,625	$1,010	$3,500	$3,500	$45,835
September	$18,000	$8,080	$2,000	$8,200	$5,750	$1,010	$3,500	$3,500	$44,960
October	$14,500	$8,080	$2,000	$8,200	$5,625	$1,010	$3,500	$3,500	$46,335
November	$14,800	$8,080	$7,100	$8,200	$5,625	$1,010	$3,500	$3,500	$51,435
December	$15,000	$8,080	$1,010	$8,200	$5,750	$1,010	$3,500	$3,500	$45,970
FY Total	$174,000	$96,080	$35,410	$98,400	$68,000	$12,120	$42,000	$42,000	$569,930
Percentage of Total	59%	17%	6%	17%	12%	2%	7%	7%	100%

The last thing I will say: You absolutely do not want to be surprised by the cost of your project. So when you consider how you will track expenses, make sure you structure the timeline of your project to include regular intervals for expense reconciliation.

For example, this is a sizable budget in the mock example. The total budget for our mock-up budget is just short of

$500,000. The fact that we are forecasting costs from January to December tells us the project will last at least one full year. If you are not tracking costs against a budget like this every month, you are just asking for trouble.

Personally, when I run a project, I am comparing the incoming expenses to the total available every week or month. If it is a long project and you wait more than a month to peek under the covers, you may get a surprise you don't really want.

The more you dig into project planning, the more you will be witness to some pretty big budgets. Be smart as you forecast the cost. Your company's leadership will appreciate your frugal nature, but do not build a budget on unreasonable figures just to make the project look less expensive. It is important to be as accurate as possible.

Inspect What You Expect

Again, the goal is not to give you a cost performance methodology, as there are plenty out there for you to research and utilize if that is the direction you want to take with the financial management aspect of your solution. Rather, this is to say, if you do nothing else, use at least two basic ways to track and communicate:

1. Calculate budget remaining
    Formula: Total Expenses Budgeted - Total Expenses YTD = Remaining Budget

    Example:

    In checking weekly expense compliance, Amber adds all the expenses that have been invested in the project thus far, $10,200. She knows the budget is $20,000. After she subtracts the amount already spent, she confirms she has

$9,800 remaining. She then looks at the individual categories of expenses to see if the $9,800 is going to be enough to cover the rest of the costs she forecasted in the plan. Good news! She estimated only another $4,000 in costs. She can now assume she will come in under budget and save the company $4,400.

2. Calculate budget remaining as a percent of total budget

Total Expenses YTD/ Total Expenses Budgeted * 100 = Percent

Example:

Michelle is the project manager on a difficult project. She is preparing a status report to give her boss information about how the project is going. He asked her to include an analysis of how the budget is covering the project and to confirm the budget is not in jeopardy of being missed.

Michelle knows the total budget is $230,000. She looks at the timeline and sees that the project is 60% of the way complete. In efforts to provide the right analysis, she totals up the costs to date, which equal $149,500. She knows that $149,500 is 65% of the budget. The numbers look close, since 40% of the work still must be completed and there are costs associated with the remaining project requirements. Michelle also knows that the expenses are spread throughout the project and thus not perfectly situated to compare to the project completion forecast. Michelle knows she has $80,500 left in the budget. She carefully reviews the remaining 40% of work and sees that most of the costs were built into the budget for upfront/starting costs and only another $60,000 costs are forecasted for the remaining work.

Michelle is not going to leave the financial success of the project just hanging there in limbo. She sends a note to the project team, letting them know that they must send her notice by the end of the day if they have an expense coming up in the project that was not part of the original budget. Thankfully, when she receives the responses from the project team, no one has anything unexpected coming. Thus, Michelle can now send her boss the analysis. She tells him that of the total $230,000 budget, 65% has been used to-date. The project still has 40% of the original requirements remaining to implement. She also informs him that the majority of the $230,000 was budgeted to cover up-front costs that have since been covered, and thus the remaining 35% of budget will more than cover the remaining expenses.

CASE STUDY:
Anonymous Entrepreneur

I worked with this entrepreneur recently, but I can't use his name or his company name.

Why? Because he lost an incredible business due to poor budgeting and financial management skills. Let's call him Andy.

Andy started a technology support service out of his garage. With little advertising, Andy was soon busy fixing Macs and PCs. He charged $125 to make a house call and $100 per hour for every hour thereafter. He worked ten hours a day to keep up with the demand.

In a typical 10-hour day, he made six house calls and brought in $900. Computers dropped off at his office for repair brought in another $300. As a one-man show, Andy was making approximately $1,200 per day —top-line sales of approximately $300,000 annually. It was a rush for a guy without experience in the business world, but the workload wasn't sustainable. He needed help.

With a modest business loan, he hired 50 technicians to cover an expanded coverage area and, within two years, grew his total sales to over $15,000,000. Andy began to advertise to small- and mid-size business owners, which increased both sales and margin. Soon he was getting calls from business owners to handle bigger jobs, including running cat-5 cable in office buildings.

Marketing to small business was turning out to be a great decision. The revenue was significantly higher per job and the margin was much better, as business owners didn't scrutinize the hourly rate as much as residential customers. The jobs were getting bigger and more complex, sometimes spanning a week or two, instead of days; these jobs required more than one technician; and they required Andy to purchase hardware and software for the clients and build those costs into the bid.

Therein lies the rub, as Andy felt he was too busy, and too successful, to slow down, invest in project management training, and adopt budget best practices. Despite the advice he seek some training, he was sure he would figure it out on his own. Budgeting couldn't be that hard, he told his business associate. And besides, he was selling plenty of new business to cover any small budgeting errors.

Andy was wrong.

This is a hard lesson for entrepreneurs to learn: Not all business is good business. Even more earth shattering: Growth can kill a company.

Andy's bookkeeper called with shocking news. The accountant pointed out that on average, Andy's business invoices were $4,500. In the course of a two-week project, labor would account for $2,700, and hardware, software, and supplies would run another $1,600. So after two weeks of work, Andy might be bringing in $200. In other words, Andy was trading residential business that had margin over 35% for corporate business yielding 4.5%. By the time the accounting team applied the indirect expenses to a project, it was in the red. Andy's great idea was costing him money.

Once a new business that isn't sufficiently capitalized begins operating on such a thin profit margin, the liquidity game intensifies. Soon the business owner has a hard time getting enough cash out of operations to support ongoing activities.

How could Andy have avoided this loss? By budgeting projects before confirming the sales price and properly managing each project to ensure the job was done without going over the budgeted amount of labor, supplies, and time.

Don't be Andy. Use the skills you are learning here to set up the right problem-solving project. If you think you need more education or training, consider building that request in as the profit to one of your future profitable problem-solving success stories.

Chapter Ten

Identify Value

Use Factor 10 Results™ to Scale Results

A key part of your plan and execution must be using the "language of value." The chief measure in your organization—no matter the initiative—is always "value." But what does that really mean?

Value can mean so many things. For our purpose, we will take a narrow view and look at it exclusively from a business perspective. I'm going to define value as "an advantage that can be expressed in terms of monetary value, utility (good will), innovation, or profit."

I have worked with problem solvers in many different industries, with a wide variety of expertise, and one consistent failing I've noticed: They tend to talk about the problem, rather than about the value of the solution. They say, "Here's how we solved the problem," but they neglect to finish the sentence with, "And that resulted in a value of X." That is like making a cake and leaving off the frosting!

Factor 10 Results™

Here is an absolutely essential concept.

Factor 10 Results™ is a proxy to help problem solvers understand how to scale (and then communicate) the enterprise value of their solution.

Factor 10 Results™ has two key tenets: Factor 10 Results and Factor 10 Reach.

Imagine that you have identified an inefficiency that affects your own office group. Solving it will provide value to your office. That's great!

But what if you imagine the results of that solution applied more broadly? What if you think about value like the CEO thinks about value?

Picture every office, company-wide, adopting your solution.

The value of your solution will be scaled and multiplied many times over. I call this Factor 10 Results™.

Your CEO will have a team of MBAs and financial experts using complicated financial ratios and modeling to scale value. To keep your project simple but still enveloped in the same language, we will use Factor 10 Results™ as a proxy—or a substitute—for the financial computations needed to project enterprise-wide value.

Surely you have heard the expression $1 + 1 = 3$.

When you think about value that matters up the chain of command, the concept of "scale" must be part of what your solution will accomplish.

In other words, if your problem-solving solution saves $100 in expenses per day, you can scale your own value in a number of ways, including something as simple as annualizing your savings over a fiscal year. After weekends and public holidays are teased out, you have approximately 250 days (give or take). If your solution saves $100 per day, multiply your daily savings by 250 business days. Your problem-solving solution will save the company $25,000. That sounds pretty good, doesn't it?

But let's not stop there. Let's assume you have 10 colleagues who save the same amount of money every day by replicating your solution. Now your solution is saving $250,000 per year.

Keep on factoring. If there are four shifts in a day with 10 people per shift, you are forecasting that your solution can save $1,000,000.

How Complicated Can It Get?

If you want to get technical (and you should), the business practitioner has a few options for calculating value across an enterprise. As I mentioned earlier, the most typical approach once you get to the MBA level or an experienced financial management level is to use financial ratios or value calculations. Let's look at some of the usual suspects to get you acquainted with the concepts and build an appreciation for the ease of using a proxy for scaling value in your project (this is not intended to be a comprehensive list):

Dealing with cash flow for start ups and entrepreneurs (Survival):

Burn Rate = Cash inflows – monthly operating costs

Days to Zero Cash = Total cash on hand/monthly burn rate = time to zero cash.

Cash Flow Coverage Ratio = Operating Cash Flows / Total Debt

Cash Flow ROI (CFROI) = Cash Flow / Market Value of Capital Employed

Operating Cash Flow / Sales Ratio = Operating Cash Flows / Sales Revenue x 100%

Ubiquitous, important, and complex (Business School 101 ... answering the question of whether to invest in the project or not):

Net Present Value (NPV) is a calculation designed to determine the present value of an investment by the discounted sum of all cash flows received from the investment or project.

If n is the number of cash flows in the list of values, the formula for NPV is:

$$NPV = \sum_{i=1}^{n} \frac{values_i}{(1 + rate)^i}$$

Internal Rate of Return (IRR) is a calculation used widely to rank various projects by profitability and potential for growth. How so, you ask? Financial managers understand that IRR is the interest rate at which the net present value of all the cash flows from a project equal zero. There are a couple ways to calculate IRR. Here is one formula:

$0 = P_0 + P_1/(1+IRR) + P_2/(1+IRR)_2 + P_3/(1+IRR)_3 + \ldots +P_n/(1+IRR)_n$

where $P_0, P_1, \ldots P_n$ equals the cash flows in periods 1, 2, . . . n, respectively; and IRR equals the project's internal rate of return.

Profitability Ratios (Is it all worth it? How your company generates earnings after expenses):

Return on Investment (ROI) = (Gains from Investment − Cost of Investment) / Cost of Investment

Return on Sales (operating margin) = EBIT / Revenue

Gross Profit Margin = Gross Profit / Revenue

ROIC = (Net Income - Dividends) / Capital Investment

EBITDA = Revenue – Expenses (excluding tax, interest, depreciation, amortization)

Return on Sales (operating margin) = EBIT / Revenue

ROE (DuPont formula) = (Net profit / Revenue) * (Revenue / Total Assets) * (Total Assets / Equity) = Net Profit Margin * Asset Turnover * Financial Leverage

Liquidity Ratios (All about the cash ... how well can your company cover near-term debt obligations?):

Cash Ratio = Cash and Cash Equivalents / Current Liabilities

The Current Ratio = Current Assets / Current Liabilities

Quick Ratio = (Current Assets - Inventories) / Current Liabilities

Working Capital (net working capital) = Current Assets - Current Liabilities

Debt Ratios (Are you in the hole? How much debt the company has on record and how much risk the debt creates for the company):

Asset Coverage Ratio = ((Total Assets – Intangible Assets) – (Current Liabilities – Short-term Debt)) / Total Debt Obligations

Debt Ratio = Liabilities / Assets

Debt Service Coverage Ratio (DSCR) = Net Operating Income / Total Debt Service

Debt-to-Equity Ratio = Liabilities / Equity

Debt-to-Income Ratio = Total Debt Payments / Total Monthly Income

Debt/EBITDA Ratio = Liabilities / EBITDA

Financial Leverage = Total Debt / Shareholders' Equity

Asset Management Ratios (how well your company can translate assets into sales):

Accounts Payable Turnover Ratio = Total Purchases / Average Accounts Payable

Asset Turnover = Revenue / Average Total Assets - *or* in days = 365 / Asset Turnover

Cash Conversion Cycle (CCC) = Days Inventory Outstanding (DIO) + Days Sales Outstanding (DSO) – Days Payable Outstanding (DPO)

Days Inventory Outstanding (DIO) = Average Inventory Level expressed in days

Days Payable Outstanding (DPO) = Accounts Payable outstanding in days

Days Sales Outstanding (DIO) is an average collection period for accounts receivable

Company and Market Value Ratios (the info your broker probably talks about):

Enterprise Value = Market Capitalization + Debt + Preferred Share Capital + Minority Interest - Cash and Cash Equivalents

PEG Ratio = Price / Earnings ÷ Annual EPS Growth

Price-to-Research Ratio = Market Capitalization / R&D Expense

Price/Book Value Ratio = Stock Price per Share / Shareholders' Equity Per Share

Price/Sales Ratio = Price per Share / Revenue per Share

Stock Price = (Assets - Liabilities + Future Earnings) / Number of Shares

In order to calculate these numbers correctly, you need access to some information that may be difficult to obtain, since some companies don't release sensitive financial data such as cost of capital, amount of working capital, labor, salary, and sales data. The good news is you don't have to let that keep you from talking about value!

Again, you don't have to use these equations in your project planning. In fact, I suggest you do not unless you are familiar with these concepts and have access to the right data for your calculations. Some of these ratios may be much more than you need at this stage, something akin to bringing a machine gun to a knife fight. Using Factor 10 Results™ as a substitute will illustrate to your management team that you understand the concept of scale and will give them a platform to formalize your projections into the right metrics and ratios for your company.

Because using a simpler substitute is a no-hassle way to get your project started, I developed a *Keep-It-Simple* approach that my clients use to remove the complexity associated with calculating value.

To determine the future value of your solution, you should consider how you will express the value. In other words, does the tangible benefit of your solution create value, create savings, or create good will? Follow along with the Factor 10 Results available on www.profitableproblemsolving.com under our *Free Stuff* section. Here are key inputs for Factor 10 Results™:

Gain: anything incremental to what you had before you introduced the problem solution.

Save: anything you can save because of the problem solution.

Utility: in economics, utility is a measure of usefulness or satisfaction by consumers. For Factor 10, we focus on the concept of satisfaction for stakeholders impacted by your problem solution.

Factor 10 *RESULTS:*

GAINS		
Self	My Gain < +>	Annualize (* number of years gain can be achieved)
Peers	Number of Peers per shift * Peer Gain <+>	Annualize (* number of years gain can be achieved)
Shift	Number of Shifts * Shift Gain <+>	Annualize (* number of years gain can be achieved)
Department	Total Department Gain	Annualize (* number of years gain can be achieved)
Division	Total Divisonal Gain	Annualize (* number of years gain can be achieved)
Enterprise	Total Enterprise Gain	Annualize (* number of years gain can be achieved)

SAVINGS		
Self	My Savings < +>	Annualize (* number of years savings can be achieved)
Peers	Number of Peers per shift * Peer Savings <+>	Annualize (* number of years savings can be achieved)
Shift	Number of Shifts * Shift Savings <+>	Annualize (* number of years savings can be achieved)
Department	Total Department Savings	Annualize (* number of years savings can be achieved)
Division	Total Divisonal Savings	Annualize (* number of years savings can be achieved)
Enterprise	Total Enterprise Savings	Annualize (* number of years savings can be achieved)

Earlier, I mentioned that Factor 10 Results™ has two key tenets: Factor 10 Results and Factor 10 Reach. We just covered the tangible value with Factor 10 Results. But what about the intangible value to the organization?

What is Intangible Value?

From a strict financial perspective, intangible value is derived from assets that are difficult to calculate, such as brand equity and the value of proprietary innovations. Most companies use a metric called Calculated Intangible Value (CIV) to determine this financial amount for their financial reporting. For our less academic purpose, we will use the term intangible more broadly and include the hard-to-calculate by-products of your solution. Some examples include:

Value of increased employee satisfaction;

Value of increased customer satisfaction; and

Value of lower employee attrition.

The biggest intangible of Factor 10 Reach is the value associated with the domino effect. You will begin (or continue) by using Profitable Problem Solving in your environment and being part of the early pioneers that start the grass roots movement toward a culture of continuous improvement.

Wait, are you saying I should hope someone copies my idea? Wouldn't that make it harder for me to take credit for my work and have a profitable experience? The answer is *no*. You absolutely want everyone to do as you do. The trick is making sure you build the concept of Factor 10 Reach into your early forecast of value, so as Tom, Dick, and Harry see your wonderful results and plan to launch a problem-solving initiative of their own, you can show the value of their solutions (which they will have their own Factor 10 Results to show) as part of your Factor 10 Reach calculation. Imagine it as the Amway of problem solving. You get credit for everyone who gets onboard after you.

Here is an easy way to think about Factor 10 Reach:

Factor 10 *REACH:*

R - Recognize value created by introducing your problem-solving initiative.

E - Expect others to follow in your path. Take credit for showing them the way.

A - Acknowledge others in the problem-solving effort (and profit because the reach was seeded in your problem-solving plan and project).

C - Connect the value of your reach and utility to your solution value.

H – Highlight the value to people around you to encourage them to try to emulate your success.

Document, Document, Document

Document every discussion, every trend, every metric, every step of your project—especially, every proof of value gained.

Documenting your project is absolutely essential.

Let me repeat that.

Documentation.

Is.

Essential.

If you are working alone to improve a simple process, a diary may be sufficient. However, for a more complex initiative that involves a team, you probably need a more dynamic way of tracking your project success. A number of free software packages, such as Basecamp, allow you to track deliverables, milestones, documents, and team members' tasks.

You need to be able to demonstrate not only "Hey, this is what I (or we) did," but also, and far more important, "and this is the Factor 10 result of that." You need to connect progress to value.

Don't neglect—and I can't emphasize this enough—the importance of testimonials. "Oh, gosh, this made my work life easier." "This new process makes me feel more productive." "I feel like I'm not spinning my wheels so much anymore." All those, coming from your fellow employees, are incredibly valuable.

But even more valuable, I believe, are testimonials from external stakeholders.

Testimonials serve as immediate evidence that you've solved the problem, they contribute to proof of "Factor 10 Results™," and they become part of your permanent record. This is a great chip in your bank for later as you make sure to gain reward for your excellent problem-solving accomplishment.

If you are regularly seeing disappointment or dissatisfaction in customers because of some particular process, you might come up with a solution and present it to management. You may not have a quantitative measure for a trend, but how about presenting a few complaints from customers?

If you have half a dozen named customers willing to be quoted saying, "I don't like your return policy, so I'm not shopping in your stores anymore," then you have evidence of a negative trend. Offer management a change in the return policy that would satisfy these customers. Then, Factor 10 it: If we project this change across other stores, other regions, other countries, how many happy customers will we save?

This can be particularly persuasive, since it is almost always less expensive to save existing customers than to acquire new ones.

Remember, you are in the process of building your own personal problem-solver portfolio, branding yourself as a problem solver, and changing the way people in your company and your industry view you.

CASE STUDY:
Nellie Greely

Serving the 150,000+ members of the world's largest independent community of SAP professionals on a small, not-for-profit budget was challenging enough for EVP and creative director Nellie Greely — but then her barely-adequate budget was cut in half.

ASUG's new CEO, Bridgette Chambers, had taken over an organization that, after consecutive years of declining revenue, was in desperate need of a turnaround. She reorganized operations, reduced budgets, and laid out ambitious objectives for her management team. Her challenge to Nellie: maintain the same level of productivity and quality, while building an improved platform for brand enhancements. And, do it with 50% less staff.

Chambers was surprised to see Nellie come into her office the very next day with a plan for maintaining the status quo with fewer resources, a new vision for managing the marketing and branding functions of the organization, and a strategy for branding that new program. That's how ASUG F.I.R.S.T. was born.

Nellie pitched ASUG F.I.R.S.T. as a new program that would reposition the marketing department more as a brand and quality assurance group, focusing on brand awareness, consistent messaging, and delivery of self-service tools to help other areas of the organization serve as subject matter experts responsible for daily content generation. Nellie's long-term vision included an online repository and project request system to streamline member communications, program and chapter activities, and national events.

Eager to brand the new department immediately, Nellie had created the "F.I.R.S.T." acronym from five of ASUG's top-level brand attributes (Frank, Independent, Relevant, Strong, and Trusted). The F.I.R.S.T identity was to be used both internally and externally to formalize the program. Nellie felt the identity would remind staff that the brand was of utmost importance and that by working to protect and extend the organization's brand equity, staff were creating long-term value for ASUG members. Tangentially, it would also serve to remind staff that before anything was distributed on behalf the organization, it was to go through ASUG F.I.R.S.T. ... well, first.

The plan was made complete with an online project request system that included service-level agreements and a brand asset library to streamline self-service aspects of the program and support functional areas in their growth and engagement goals.

Confronted with the complexity and scale of her budget issue, it would have been easy for Nellie to think small. Instead, she thought BIG about how to turn a short-term challenge into a long-term win, not only for the organization, but also for her as a leader within the organization.

While the original savings were important, Nellie was able to use Factor 10 Results™ to scale the savings into much larger returns for ASUG. By building big and connecting the solution to value for the organization, she became known as a profitable problem solver. She leveraged her success with ASUG F.I.R.S.T. to build a portfolio of successes that aided ASUG in its swift transformation back to a powerhouse of influence and credibility within the SAP ecosystem. With a little strategy, a lot of creativity, and an unwavering focus on execution, what at first seemed like an insurmountable task became a positive reality. As Nelson Mandela once famously said, "It always seems impossible 'til it's done."

Chapter Eleven

Take Action

Execute with Confidence

Profitable Problem Solving is flexible.

There's no strict manual for it, no overly rigorous rules, just six simple steps to be performed in whatever style makes sense to you and your company culture.

And that's what makes it so great! I've designed the strategy to be agile enough that any employee or any company can embrace, customize, adopt, and adapt it to create a perfect fit.

So how will you make that flexible, agile approach work for you? By this point, you have completed five of the six PROFIT steps. You are ready to dig into the most exciting part of your problem-solving quest. You're ready to TAKE ACTION.

There are two important aspects to TAKE ACTION. The first is making sure that if you need permission (and remember that asking for forgiveness instead of permission is not always a bad option) or sponsorship for your program, then it should be the first important phase of your TAKE ACTION step.

Remember the Profitable Problem-solving Matrix we used in the early stages? If you are in the green, you are likely clear to make your plan and move forward. However, if you are in a yellow zone, you should carefully weigh the importance of presenting your plan to the right member of your leadership team.

Selling Your Vision

In your current position, you may have the authority to direct people to work on your problem-solving initiative. Or, you may not.

If your project plan requires others to actively participate or budgets the labor dollars of anyone beyond yourself, you need to have the right sponsorship. You want to present your project plan (and your next best alternative) to the right person.

Building Your Presentation

Reach back into your memory and pull out those details we discussed in Step 3: Outline Solution. We explored some planning requirements in detail. Dust these off and use them in your PowerPoint or written presentation. The key ones to include are:

Problem Statement
Solution Statement
Your Motivation for Solving this Problem
Supporting Data
Cost Forecast
Value
Factor 10 Value
Next Steps

Remember that Audience You Assembled?

Earlier in the six steps, as you built your plan, you considered the audience you would need. Now make sure you reflect on the audience you planned to target, as many of those same people may be the right audience for you to present your plan to and seek sponsorship and authorization to move forward. The right audience should include the following types of roles (and, yes, one person may fill multiple roles):

Your Biggest Fan: It goes without saying that you need someone in the audience who will go to bat for you and talk about your potential, your previous success, and your intentions.

The Banker: You need someone in the audience who can authorize the company to cover the costs you have forecasted in your project, if you lack that authority directly.

The Decision Maker: The decision maker and the banker may often be the same person; however, not 100 percent of the time. If you require project approval from someone who would still have to seek further approval for the costs, consider inviting them both professionals to your presentation.

The Big Cheese: You are looking for exposure and opportunity. Inviting someone up the chain is a great way to get some exposure to your go-getting, can-do attitude. Be careful not to ruffle feathers if your environment is a political one … but don't miss the chance to show off your ability to assess and plan for improvement.

If you have other considerations, such as a safety officer, legal counsel, or technology expert, make sure you include them so you can pitch your solution and close for a decision in one meeting.

One final hint: If you have multiple people in the audience, make sure you have prepped those you wish to contribute. Don't invite someone and just hope they will say the right thing when you cue them. Invest the time to prep them and gain confirmation that they are onboard with your plan. This is a great way to begin to flex your leadership muscles in your problem-solving project.

Close Big

Finally, presentation in hand, you must get in there and **close big**.

Successful salespeople live by this maxim: *If you don't ask for it, you aren't going to get it.*

Simply presenting an idea is not the same as asking decision makers for a "yes" or a "no."

If you present your plan and just say, "Thank you. Do you have any questions?", then you may very well get this response, "Nope, no questions. I'll think about it. Thanks."

But if you present your plan and ask whether the decision makers intend to support it, you have made it very clear that there is a question on the table. "Yes? No? Or next best alternative?"

Great news …you have now learned the PROFIT steps to solving the problem. Let's start to wrap up your problem-solving education with the next two steps. They are purely about you—*making the success profitable for you.*

Problem Statement – Looking For Trouble

Research Trends – Build your Case

Outline Solution – Planning for Success

Forecast Cost – Be Smart with Resources

Identify Value – Use Factor 10 to Scale Value

Take Action – Execute with Confidence

Take Credit – The Profit is Yours

Learn How Personal PR is the Next
Step in Profitable Problem Solving

CASE STUDY:
Jack Welch and General Electric

During Jack Welch's 20 years at the helm of General Electric, from 1981 to 2001, he evolved GE from an old-economy manufacturer into a modern conglomerate. The company's value rose an amazing 4,000%, to a value of $410 billion.[12]

When he took over as GE's youngest-ever CEO in 1981, Welch initiated a restructuring plan. He instituted massive job cuts (a full 25% of GE's worldwide workforce), insisted that GE would rank either first or second in every segment, and sold off hundreds of unprofitable or underperforming businesses. Welch had inherited 29 layers of hierarchy; he transformed GE into an informal company in which every employee felt empowered to solve problems.

He might not have used these exact words, but the corporate culture that Welch developed was the archetype of the Profitable Problem Solving culture. His trademark leadership style gave his managers wide latitude to build their units in entrepreneurial fashion. He truly created a culture of continuous improvement. In his own words, "The individual is the fountainhead of creativity and innovation, and we are struggling to get all of our people to accept the countercultural truth that often the best way to manage people is just to get out of their way. Only by releasing the energy and fire of our employees can we achieve the decisive, continuous productivity advantages that will give us the freedom to compete and win in any business anywhere on the globe."

Known for being brutally direct, Welch refused to stand for muddy thinking. He abolished five-year plans, since he believed that any person who claimed to be able to plan five years into the future was a "bullshitter." [13] He demanded clear, simple explanations of the challenges his people faced and their plans for overcoming them.

Are these strategies that will work for every company? Of course not. Not only was Welch a genius leader, but he had the good fortune of taking over a massive company that operated a vast number of businesses with more than 400,000 employees. In such a huge enterprise, it is not totally surprising that Welch was able to improve operations by removing the bottom 120,000 of GE's worldwide employees — and, by massively rewarding the top 20%.

Not every CEO has Welch's talents — or the opportunity to lead a General Electric. But we still all have a lot to learn from Welch's success and his style.

His no-nonsense approach to action and execution was characterized by a few best practices that became his trademark: business is simple, so don't make it overly complicated; face reality, and don't fear change; fight bureaucracy; use the brains of your workers; and discover who has the best ideas and put those ideas into practice!

Whatever the size of the corporation, imbedding these characteristics into the organization's DNA are sure to encourage creativity, innovation, and continuous improvement.

Chapter Twelve

Take Credit

The Profit is Yours

Should you be shy about proposing a problem-solving initiative to management? After you've successfully finished and documented a project, should you hesitate to announce, "Look at what I've accomplished!"

In a word: *No.*

Should you be ashamed to expect a return in exchange for the value your problem-solving provides to your organization?

In three words: *No, no, no!*

After all, what is the underlying premise of our economic system?

I provide value to you, in exchange for which you provide value to me.

Every employee, manager, and leader, at every level of the company, is engaged in a mutually beneficial transaction with the organization, its stakeholders, and its shareholders. That way, everyone benefits. That's our system.

If you are solving problems to improve your company's profitability but you are not profiting personally, then I hope you really enjoy what you're doing—because you are giving it away.

You Deserve to Be Rewarded

How should you expect to profit from your problem-solving initiatives?

One of the most fascinating things about profitable problem solving is that different problem solvers may want different rewards. Not only that, but the same problem solver may have a different reward in mind as a result of different initiatives. The problem solver can adjust the desired reward as she continues to move forward in her career.

You have a certain amount of flexibility in deciding what's valuable to you. Give a lot of thought to the value that you want to link to each problem you solve. Consider the value of a portfolio of problems that you've taken on over the course of a fiscal quarter or a year.

Your reward may be a raise, or a promotion, or additional responsibility in your day-to-day job. Perhaps the problem-solving employee has something specific in mind, such as the opportunity to be considered for an educational opportunity. If the company offers tuition for a master's degree program, a successful problem-solving initiative gives the employee the opportunity to say, "Look at what I've accomplished for the company. If you invest in me, imagine how much more valuable I can be."

Another form of personal reward, a benefit for yourself in the long run, might be as simple as recognition as a successful entrepreneurial problem solver ... which would lead to being trusted to take the initiative on another, more complex problem ... which, in turn, would lead to greater rewards in the future. Do not underestimate the importance of recognition.

Our lives change. Our careers are like roller coasters, climbing and dipping, but hopefully all in a generally upward trajectory. What you want today is different than what you are going to want tomorrow.

As your career progresses, you'll likely find yourself tackling more complex, more difficult challenges. As the problems become bigger, so should the reward. Be patient enough to start small, but keep your gaze on the horizon.

Make sure you are constantly attaching rewards to your problem-solving achievements. It might be a tangible reward like a raise or a promotion, but just as valuable, in the long run, might be one more sparkle on your personal brand as a successful, entrepreneurial problem solver.

Whatever the reward you desire, know this: The key to being rewarded is self-promotion.

Should I Really Promote Myself? Is that Okay?

It is not only okay, it is critical. You won't get what you don't ask for. No one else is likely to ask or promote on your behalf.

When you were interviewing for your job with this company, you weren't shy about your accomplishments at your last job. Use the problems you've solved at your current company in exactly the same way. "I knew how to solve this problem because I've dealt with issues of optimization in this industry," you might say. "I (or "my team and I") created improved productivity, and that experience has given me new insights into these functions of the company. Now, I'm ready to apply these insights to tackle a slightly larger problem."

In a division or company with hundreds or thousands of employees, it is virtually impossible for a manager to pick the entrepreneurial problem solver out of the crowd. So, help her out.

Give her a hand.

Promote yourself!

Good managers love the entrepreneurial employee who walks in with confidence to present a problem and its solution. After all, part of the credit for the problem solver's success devolves to the manager. Here are some ways you can self-promote:

> Make sure to build that portfolio of accomplishments we have mentioned throughout the book. If you are going to self-promote, you need a list of accomplishments to mention.

> Build an elevator pitch for your top success stories. Instead of just reporting that everything is going well with your project, be prepared to share a concise and gripping story about your accomplishment that highlights your leadership, the value of the project, and how the value will scale (Factor 10 Results™) to drive more value across the entire enterprise.

> Don't be afraid to do a victory dance. When you have a great win, celebrate it in an email to your boss (and their boss) and make sure the celebratory note lists your success and the value of the success.

> Post & Promote. In today's social world, you have many social networks available to you to highlight accomplishments and shape your personal brand. Consider sharing with any internal network your company sponsors that is on the lookout for newsworthy activities and accomplishments in the workplace.

Measure Success and Personal Profit

For the entrepreneurial problem solver, beauty is in the eye of the beholder.

As an individual problem solver, it truly is up to you to decide what reward you want as a result of your problem-solving initiative and how you measure failure or success.

If your aim is an increase in compensation or a promotion to a particular position, that's easy to measure.

However, if your aim is something less tangible—recognition, improvement of your brand within the company, certain amenities associated with your employment—then it's up to you to decide whether you're satisfied with the benefits you gain from your initiative.

A company will always pay for value (assuming they agree you delivered value), but if you find yourself thinking, "The success of my project, and the value (particularly the Factor 10 Results™) to the organization, deserved a more substantial reward than what I received," then one of two things went wrong.

First, you may have failed to properly demonstrate the value of your project up front, and thus the need to reward you with something substantial did not make sense to your management team. This is why Factor 10 Results™ is so important. It automatically extrapolates for you and provides clear evidence of the value you've achieved for the company.

The second possible mistake, you may have failed to make a clear connection between the value you've provided and the reward you expect for it. This should have been cemented as part of your planning and presentation.

At the risk of unfairly generalizing, I believe that women, in particular, are notoriously poor at asking for a reward. We are excellent at pointing out problems, we are highly effective problem solvers, and we tend to expect that if we solve a problem, then top management will recognize our contributions and reward us for them.

To which I say: *Crap.*

Here's what you need to do.

This is not a suggestion.

You *need* to do this.

When you are first proposing a problem-solving initiative, tell management, "Hey, listen, here's my plan. I am motivated to solve this problem because I want to do good things for the company and I know the company will do good things for me in return. Here's the Factor 10 Results™ the company is going to get from it. I'm going to execute the plan, and when it's done and reaping Factor 10 Results to the company, then I'm expecting ..."

And here, fill in the blank. "I am going to want more responsibility as a result of solving this problem." "I'm going to want a raise." "I'm going to want a promotion." Or, "I know these particular projects are coming up. Based on the success of the problem solving I'm doing now, I want you to start thinking of me as the leader of these future projects."

Some people worry that they'll become scorned as ruthless self-promoters.

I have one word for that attitude: *More crap!*

The people who worry about being known as ruthless self-promoters are the people who watch everyone else getting promoted.

Handle your self-promotion carefully, of course — thoughtfully, gracefully, and smoothly. Refine your communication skills. But don't be afraid to promote yourself, because no one else will do it for you.

What About the Pirates?

As we discussed earlier, there are folks out there who will seek to take credit for an original idea that belongs to another. As you self-promote, keep in mind the Factor 10 Results™ concept.

"When we solve this problem," you'll say, "there will be an impact not only in this one office or factory or division, but right across the organization."

This is a great way to insulate yourself against someone who may be only tangentially involved in your problem-solving initiative, but who is a better self-promoter than you. By declaring the Factor 10 Reach of your initiative (think back to Chapter 10), you let people throughout the organization know it was you who identified the problem, came up with the solution, and expected others to follow in your footsteps.

In effect, you'll be saying, "I set the dominos in motion!" You'll be ensuring that credit stays where credit belongs: with *you*.

To Close the Loop, Do Your Own Post-mortem

When your initiative is finished, perform a personal post-mortem.

Ask yourself, *How could I have done better?*

Did I analyze all the trends correctly?

Could I have built a better team and a better audience?

And, most important of all, *Did I build my personal strategy correctly, connect my work to value, and connect it to my own reward?*

Why? Why would I take the time to do such a review? Simple, the review is the path to building a strong portfolio of accomplishments. With a post-mortem, you will learn what to do again and what to adjust when building problem-solving plans.

Take the time to do the review and consider it a best practice for success. Imagine you are watching the game tapes from your last championship game and learn from the entire experience.

CASE STUDY:
John Chen and Sybase

When John Chen took over the helm as CEO of Sybase in 1998, the Silicon Valley-based technology giant had seen far better days. Formerly a fierce competitor of Oracle, Sybase had failed to innovate into the enterprise application market, and by 1998, it was — by Chen's reckoning — "a very, very dead company." [14]

From near death, Chen and his team resurrected Sybase and took it to a valuation of $5.8 billion and acquisition by SAP.

How did Chen "turn the battleship" that was Sybase? In structural terms, Chen developed and adapted a new vision, which he called *the unwired platform.* He took a company that had been a client-server database company, and — believing that mobile enterprise computing was destined to be the next really big thing — he positioned Sybase in high-growth areas like analytics, mobile middleware, and mobile services. Sybase became "an enabler of the unwired enterprise."

But just as important — or even more so — Chen brought with him a style of empowering his people that nurtured a culture of continuous improvement.

Chen says, "The key was that we had a team of people who were willing to do this, who would hang in there. Because there were going to be a lot of ups and downs." Chen has talked extensively about how important a problem-solving culture is to a successful corporate turnaround. "A turnaround culture must be positive," he's said.

"Employees need to have the hunger — and confidence — to get things done. Everyone needs the same single-minded desire to win."

Part of creating and driving that problem-solving culture is making sure everyone shares a common language of value. Chen is known for encouraging his team to bring solutions to the table for discussion and for nurturing a culture of empowerment as the team searches for solutions. "When you only talk about the problems," says Chen, "you drag everyone down. Energy dissipates; hopelessness reigns. [The culture that is needed is] one that focuses on fixing things and finding solutions, *not* on the obstacles before you."

"If you empower employees," says Chen, "they will speak out on bad decisions or take the initiative to solve problems. No matter what their level, everyone can make a difference. They can help evangelize to customers, engage with partners, reduce costs and waste, and help on your overall strategy."

"Creating this openness requires a few things. Leaders need to listen and be humble ... Besides, you're already paying your employees! Why not let them take initiative — you'll get the results." 15

Chen created immense value for Sybase's shareholders and employees, and by doing so, he also created huge reward for himself.

With Sybase's astonishing turnaround in his portfolio of achievements, Chen had gained a reputation as a turnaround specialist extraordinaire. Based on his ability to brand himself (and accomplishments) as successful turnaround artillery, he is a highly sought after hired gun. Next stop? In 2013, he took over the CEO-ship of embattled Blackberry, with a reported compensation package of $88 million. [16]

Turning around Blackberry is a huge challenge — but I wouldn't bet against Chen to nurture a successful profitable problem-solving culture at Blackberry, just like he did at Sybase.

Chapter Thirteen

Personal PR is the Next Step
in Profitable Problem Solving

Profitable Problem Solving has a lot in common with shampooing your hair.

Huh? What's Bridgette talking about now?

Well, what does it say on a shampoo bottle?

Rinse and repeat.

Here's what I suggest. Once you've identified a problem, solved it, and self-promoted ... do it again.

Problem solving is a skill, and like any skill, you need to sharpen it.

This is about starting small, learning as you go, building your own problem-solving discipline, learning from every experience, achieving a reward for yourself, and doing it again ... and again ... and again ... until you've built an astonishing portfolio of accomplishments.

Becoming a problem solver is not something you do once, and then settle back, cross your arms, and enjoy watching the world bow before you. It is something you learn to do and get better at. You build a portfolio of successful experiences, which will vouch for your ability to take on the next more complex role, and then the next, and so on.

This is why garnering testimonials along the way is so important. You might think about the details of your initiative as the skeleton of your project, but testimonials are the flesh, blood, and beating heart that bring it to life.

Build that portfolio of accomplishments, including glowing testimonials, and you'll have proof that you've been successful in getting traction. You'll have the tools you need to get people to buy into your next initiative. You'll gain a reputation as a serial problem solver.

Brand Your Way to the Top

Problem Solving is a Numbers Game

Think of that problem-solving portfolio we keep talking about as you're building a resume-in-process. When you are ready to brand yourself, this portfolio is the source of your great stories. You may use it to seek another position within your current company, to apply for a job with a new organization, or to lay the groundwork for a new career as a turnaround consultant.

I've known incredibly smart people whose resumes are yawners. *I had this job, I earned that degree.* But they're too timid to tell the world: *I accomplished this, I achieved that!*

Consider two workers.

Joe has solved 20 complex, difficult problems and yielded immense Factor 10 Results™ to the company—but it's a well-kept secret.

Mary has solved three medium-grade problems, but everyone from the CEO on down knows about her accomplishments.

Which of those, do you think, is going to be branded as a tremendous problem solver, a budding change management specialist?

Joe may actually provide more value to his company, but Mary is going to be the hero, and likely the next to be promoted.

No matter what direction you see your career taking you, even if you have no interest in becoming a change management specialist, problem solving should be part of your professional profile.

When you interview for a job with another company or in another industry, or just throw your hat in the ring for a higher job at your own company, you'll be asked, "Tell me about a problem you've solved." If you've built a stunning reputation … if you can present a brimming portfolio of problems tackled and solved … if you can show how you've grown into a problem-solving dynamo … then you'll be the rock star.

Your Personal Brand

You want to achieve a reputation as a problem solver within your own organization, but your ultimate goal should be to brand yourself independently from your company. Why? You need to have a brand in the market to stand on when you are ready to make a move in your career.

Building and enhancing your brand begins by understanding your brand. Ask yourself what I call the Three W's of your brand:

Who am I?

What do I do?

Why am I relevant?

Once you can answer those three Ws of your brand, make sure you have thought about the key fundamental elements of your brand, as all of these elements will eventually support the brand you envision.

What are your core values? What do you hold dear?

Example:

> *My core values include integrity, full transparency, and keeping my promises.*

What is your vision?

Example:

> *My vision is to contribute to solutions and companies that generate value for their customers and benefit the community they serve.*

What are your long-term goals?

Example:

> *I plan to hold an executive position, making at least double the income I currently earn and garner enough empowerment that I can solve problems and drive value for my company.*

What are your best strengths or attributes?

Example:

> *I bring many strengths to the table, including my leadership skills, communication skills, team building skills, and financial management skills.*

How is your brand different or valuable? How will you differentiate yourself in a crowd?

Example:

> *I bring a unique combination of hard driving leadership mixed with a keen ability to build strong teams. I am unique in my ability to drive a team of high performers to achieve ambitious goals.*

How does problem solving fit into your brand?

Example:

> *I am an accomplished problem solver focused on delivering value to the company I represent. I do not see problems; I see opportunities. I have a proven strategy that increases the probability of my success (of course you do, after reading this book) and includes a sharp focus on delivering value beyond my area of responsibility and benefiting the entire company.*

What is the Difference in Marketing and Branding?

Great question. Your brand is your identity. Marketing is the voice and activities you employ to sell your brand. Once you have completed the brand exercise outlined above, you can begin to see how your brand is forming and evolving.

When looking for examples of genius in the marketplace, the search stops with Jeff Bezos, Founder and CEO of Amazon.com. Jeff was asked about branding and replied, "A brand for your company is like a reputation for a person. You earn reputation by trying to do hard things." I like the way Jeff put it because it connects brand to reputation and that connection is where you make your brand work for you, assuming your reputation is a good one. That is what you are building upon in Profitable Problem Solving™.

So I have this brand, how do I market myself? This is formal, social side of self-promotion. Consider the following when marketing your brand as a problem solver to the market at large:

Social networks like LinkedIn, Facebook, Twitter, and AboutMe are great places to create a profile that fits your brand and keep it current with great updates about recent accomplishments. One important thing to note about social media, do not co-mingle your personal social profiles with your business profile. A Facebook page with images of you having a great time with friends at a bar is not going to be a great place to build credibility as a problem solver. If you use Facebook or Twitter, or whatever the network for personal reasons, I suggest you lock up the privacy standards and keep it tucked away. You may even need to rethink what you post in general. Remember, once it is out there, it is a potential impact to your brand; how good or bad the impact is based on what you allow to be posted.

Are you a blogger yet? Consider a blog about your specialty skill or industry. You should follow all of the disclosure rules your employer has set forth for employees on social media; however, once clear of any violations, sharing your problem-solving experiences on a blog is a great way to create a virtual audience and raise the credibility and relevancy of your personal brand.

Other options include launching a website of your own, establishing an expanded network throughout your industry, and taking advantage of opportunities to write magazine articles and give speeches. You want to take the time to promote yourself for industry-wide recognition, and be prepared to take references and testimonials with you when you go somewhere else.

CASE STUDY:
Patrick Doyle and Domino's Pizza

In the 1980s, Domino's Pizza was the fastest growing franchise chain in history, but by 2010, when Patrick Doyle was promoted to president and CEO, the company was in desperate need of a turnaround.

"We were the 30-minute guys," says Doyle. "We were going to get a pizza to you that's going to be okay, but we're going get it to you quickly. And that just stopped working."

Customers were no longer willing to settle for a pizza that was just okay, no matter how fast it arrived.

"We realized there was no conflict between delivering pizza quickly to people and making it great." [17]

Under Doyle's leadership, the chain dumped its existing pizza recipe, started over from scratch, and spent millions of dollars creating a better pizza. That was a bold enough move. But the way Doyle announced the new Domino's pizza was truly courageous. He gave the business world a lesson in how to fail in public.

Doyle started out by making an admission that very few corporate leaders have ever been willing to make: *Our pizza just isn't very good.* Focus groups and falling sales had been providing clear evidence of that to Domino's management for several years, but Doyle insisted on shining the brightest possible light on Domino's lackluster product.

In a well-planned, thoroughly integrated advertising, social media, and public relations campaign, Doyle communicated honestly and transparently with his company's customers. Keep in mind, the personal touch from Doyle in these commercials and interactions not only helped the company emerge from an underperforming position, it branded him as the true problem solver and catalyst for change. His brand was growing as the Domino's brand was healing.

The campaign succeeded for a number of reasons. Domino's waited patiently, not launching until its new pizza was beating every other product in the category in taste tests.

Domino's message was focused: *Our old product was bad, but the new product is awesome.*

The company so thoroughly trashed its old product that the only possible direction was forward.

They paid plenty of attention to internal public relations, and they offered pricing incentives to encourage customers to try the new product. [18]

The new Domino's product seems to have been positive for fans of fast, tasty pizza. But it's also been a winner for shareholders, as Domino's shares surged from $12 to more than $75 from 2010 to 2013.

And for Patrick Doyle? As leader — and public face — of Domino's Pizza, Doyle has gained a reputation as a creative manager, bold leader, and a phenomenally successful turnaround specialist.

Final Thoughts to the Reader

We've just completed a journey that should have built on the special DNA that belongs only to a special breed of person—those who seek to make things better than they find them.

Not everyone is like you. You fix things that others would walk around and avoid. Kudos to you and that fire inside you that compels you to use your problem-solving skills to benefit yourself, your company, and your community. Whatever tomorrow is will be our collective legacy, and I know that with people like you out there, it will be a bright day and a legacy we will look upon with pride.

Now you are armed with a strategy for selecting and solving problems. You have the insight to build and polish your brand and then market yourself in a way that can help you realize your goals and dreams. These strategies have worked for me and many others. By sharing these principles with you, I dream that your future will be firmly in your grasp.

I challenge you to make this a persistent state. Use these strategies, and then share the outcome on profitableproblemsolving.com/share/. Let the others know what you've learned and achieved. I will compile your experiences and share them as a community portfolio of success stories. You can share your stories and gain some insight from the stories others have posted. This is your invitation to our grassroots approach to Profitable Problem Solving.

Final Thoughts to the
CEO and Top Management Team

You have the best job of all. Every single day that I've had the pleasure to serve shareholders and a board of directors has been an exceptional day.

You are the driving strategic force for the entire company and the brand custodian to the outside world. Your legacy will be filled with accomplishments, failures, ups, downs ... and all the usual CEO artifacts.

The great CEOs are the superstars who build a legacy filled with sustained profitability, market-changing innovations that create competitive advantage, and enduring corporate cultures that fuel continuous improvement. You safeguard your company from disruption and loss, and you provide unapologetic market leadership.

That type of legacy comes from an empowerment of your most valuable asset: your people. You must empower and incent people to give you the best of their talents and minds every day. The CEOs who have blazed a trail before us—or those who are re-writing history in front our eyes today—are the ones who do not flinch when it comes to empowering people.

The task ahead, the steps to transforming your culture into a persistent state of continuous improvement, is so critical that it would take an entire book to outline the strategies and best practices with which you must arm yourself as you move forward. And guess what? That is exactly what is coming next. Watch for *Profitable Problem Solving for Executives*.

Acknowledgements

1 http://www.gallup.com/poll/143573/Entrepreneur-Mindset-Common-China.aspx

2 http://www.statisticbrain.com/startup-failure-by-industry/

3 http://smallbusiness.chron.com/businesses-high-failure-rates-61640.html

4 http://www.sba.gov/content/small-business-trends

5 http://www.big4.com/andersen/protiviti-responds-to-tough-financial-crisis-now-more-bullish-471/

6 http://content.time.com/time/magazine/article/0,9171,2022624,00.html

7 http://en.wikipedia.org/wiki/Instagram

8 http://en.wikipedia.org/wiki/MOPP

9 http://adage.com/article/news/mcdonald-s-1-rank-millennials/240497

10 http://usatoday.com/story/money/cars/2015/03/13/gm-melton-brooke-lawsuit-settle-ignition-switch-death-recall/70271724

11 http://www.forbes.com/sites/joannmuller/2014/05/28/exclusive-inside-mary-barras-urgent-mission-to-fix-gm/

12 http://niccollsanddimes.com/2012/04/22/the-general-electric-turnaround-why-we-cant-all-be-jack-welsh

13 http://www.casestudyinc.com/ge-turnaround-and-jack-welch-leadership

14 http://www.itworld.com/article/2758499/mobile/Sybase-ceo-john-chen--take-of-a-turnaround.html

[15] https://www.linkedin.com/pulse/20141027115155-14119785-the-keys-to-executing-a-turnaround-the-right-way

[16] http://www.canadianbusiness.com/business-news/new-blackberry-chairman-ceo-john-chen-receives-88-million-pay-package

[17] http://www.foxbusiness.com/business-leaders/2014/04/09/deep-dish-dominos-ceo-talks-turnaround-success

[18] http://spinsucks.com/communication/eleven-reasons-dominos-turnaround-campaign-worked

[19] http://en.wikipedia.org/wiki/Steve_Ballmer

[20] http://hiring.monster.com/hr/hr-best-practices/workforce-management/hr-management-skills/business-success.aspx

[21] http://www.vanityfair.com/news/2012/07/Microsoft-downfall-emails-steve-ballmer

[22] http://www.forbes.com/sites/stevedenning/2014/01/15/making-sense-of-zappos-and-holacracy

To contact Bridgette Chambers:
info@profitableproblemsolving.com

Profitableproblemsolving.com